CONTENTS

PREFACE   *Arthur Seldon*   7

THE AUTHORS   10

SIGNIFICANCE: *The importance of the proposals for the
                  British Reader*   between pp. 45-46

PART I: DEMOCRACY AND KEYNESIAN CONSTITUTIONS:
           POLITICAL BIASES AND ECONOMIC CONSEQUENCES   11
                  *James M. Buchanan
                        and
                  Richard E. Wagner*

A. Visions of the Economic Order: Classical and
     Keynesian   13
       From Classical stability to Keynesian instability   13

B. The Idealised Environment for Keynesian
     Economic Policy   14
       Keynes's defective assumptions   16

C. Keynesian Presuppositions, Democratic Politics,
     and Economic Policy   18
       Market and political competition: similarities
         and essential differences   18
       Budgets: political gains and losses   19
       (i)   Budget surpluses and democratic politics   20
       (ii) Budget deficits and democratic politics   22
       (iii) Keynesian economics in political democracy   23

D. The Destructive, Self-fulfilling Character of the
     Keynesian Political Biases   24
       Hayek's analysis of the impact of inflation   26

E. Conclusion   27

PART II: KEYNES'S LEGACY TO GREAT BRITAIN:
           'FOLLY IN A GREAT KINGDOM'   29
                  John Burton

A. Britain's Changing Fiscal History   31
       The pre-Keynesian budgetary record   31
       The Keynesian budgetary record   33
       The displacement hypothesis   35

B. The Pre-Keynesian British Fiscal Constitution 36
    The conventions of the fiscal constitution in
       19th-century Britain 37
    The cohesion and functioning of the British
       19th-century fiscal constitution 39
    The establishment of the balanced-budget rule in
       19th-century Britain 41
    The pressures towards excessive expenditure and
       deficit finance in the 19th century 44

C. The Presuppositions of John Maynard Keynes 47
    (1) 'The public interest' 47
    (2) The philosopher-king hypothesis of the British
       ruling élite 48
    (3) The élite's power of persuasion 49
       The Bloomsbury View 49
       The dentist model of the economic adviser 50

D. The Keynesian British Fiscal Constitution—in
    Theory 51
       (i) Meade 52
       (ii) Dalton 53
       (iii) Kaldor 54
       Conclusion 55

E. The Keynesian British Fiscal Constitution—in
    Reality 56
       Keynesian presuppositions v. Whitehall/
       Westminster realpolitik 57

F. The Failure of Remedial Measures 61
       Plowden and PESC, 1961: an attempt at reform 61
       The crisis measures of 1976 67
       A conversion of the policy-makers? 69
       An evaluation of the prospects 70
       The November 1977 'reflation' 72

G. Conclusion: 'Folly in a Great Kingdom' 73

PART III: CONSTITUTIONAL OPTIONS FOR FISCAL CONTROL 77
J. M. Buchanan, J. Burton
and
R. E. Wagner

A. Fatalism v. Reform 79
       Force the helmsman to stop fiddling with the
       tiller? 80

B. Concrete Proposals for the Reform of the British
    Fiscal-Monetary Constitution   81
    1. A combined budget statement   81
    2. Re-adopt the balanced-budget principle   81
    3. Automatic adjustment towards budget balance   82
    4. Orderly transition to full implementation   83
    5. Waiver in national emergency   83
    6. Conditions for monetary stability   83

C. Unfounded Fears   84

QUESTIONS FOR DISCUSSION   87

FURTHER READING   88

TABLES

I. The pre-Keynesian British budgetary record,
    selected years, 1790-1935   32

II. The Keynesian British budgetary record, annual
    figures, 1946-76   34

III. The 'hump effect': PESC projections of the rate of
    growth of government expenditure, 1970-71 to
    1979-80   65

[5]

PREFACE

The *Hobart Papers* are intended to contribute a stream of authoritative, independent and lucid analyses to the understanding and application of economics to private and government activity. Their characteristic theme has been the optimum use of scarce resources and the extent to which it can best be achieved in markets within an appropriate framework of laws and institutions or, where markets cannot work or have disproportionate defects, by better methods with relative advantages or less decisive defects. Since the alternative to the market is in practice the state, and both are imperfect, the choice between them is made on the judgement of the comparative consequences of market failure and government failure.

Markets have to work in an environment of laws and institutions; laws are made by government, and institutions are largely shaped by it. The most important part of this environment has long been thought to be in the realm of money and taxes. The provision of a monetary system to facilitate exchange in the market, the creation of a structure of taxes to finance government with the least possible adverse effect on effort and enterprise, and, not least, matching government income with expenditure in its budget have all been thought to be fundamental tasks of government. The purpose of government was thought to be to do what was necessary to help the economic system in which men come together as buyers and sellers to work as smoothly as possible and no more, apart from the direct provision of 'public goods' that could not be supplied in the market.

Forty years ago this notion of the function of government was contested by J. M. Keynes, who claimed that the economic system required more from government than the creation of the framework of laws and institutions because it would settle down into a state in which less than all resources were employed. He taught that government would have to undertake the new function of using its budget to run not only its own activities, but also to maintain the whole economic system in full employment by off-setting its fluctuations with opposite fluctuations in budgetary expansion or contraction of money and credit. He contended that only in this way would it be possible to maintain an otherwise freely working economic system in a more or less stable condition without disturbing fluctuations.

[7]

This diagnosis of the working of the economic system and the remedy for its supposed instability was questioned from the very beginning by economists whose doubts were not paid much attention,[1] perhaps because the Keynesian revolution of 1936 was soon followed by six years of war, by 10 years of recovery from war, and by a further decade in which the Keynesian prescription seemed to have worked in maintaining full employment, a more or less steady though not spectacular rate of growth, and what now seems to be only very modest inflation. In recent years the Keynesian economic diagnosis has come under increasing criticism and is now accepted by fewer economists and rejected by more than at any time since its origin.

Hobart Paper 78 presents a new critique of Keynes. It is concerned not so much with the accuracy of his economics as with the realism of his politics. Its subject is not whether Keynes was right as a technical economist in establishing the instability and inherent under-employment of the market economy, but whether the instrument he devised to make it stable, budget deficits, could be used by politicians in representative democracy to serve the purpose he intended. Even a technically perfect solution devised by economists may be damaging if it exposes them to irresistible importunities and sectional pressures to misuse it. Keynes 'turned the politicians loose' (Part I, p. 27): he gave them the excuse to overspend, overborrow and create money; and they have run amok.

This is the critique of Keynesianism made by Professors J. M. Buchanan and Richard E. Wagner of the USA in Part I of this *Hobart Paper*. Their argument is adapted to illuminate the post-war history of British economic policy by John Burton in Part II. And in Part III they come together to indicate the lessons that should be learnt and applied.

The conclusion they reach is no less than that government must again be controlled by rules to prevent it from using and abusing the method of budget deficits that Keynes's analysis seemed to validate, and his personal authority persuaded government to adopt—although they did not require much persuasion. And, to make certain that government does not avoid the rules, the authors suggest that they be put into writing and be made part of the constitution.

[1] The leading dissident was Professor F. A. Hayek whose writings on the Keynesian debate are indicated in *A Tiger by the Tail*, Hobart Paperback 4, IEA, 1972, 2nd Edition 1978.

Hobart Paper 78 is, in effect, an application of the relatively new economics of politics, of which Professor Buchanan is a Founding Father. (Another is Professor Gordon Tullock, who outlined its main propositions in *The Vote Motive*, 1976.) Economists have moved from what was considered their sphere of interest, the exchange economy, into the activities of government itself. Government is no longer regarded as an external and benign provider of the legal/institutional environment, but as a direct activist in the economy, which it is induced by pressures and its own interest to manipulate for its advantage. In the jargon, government is regarded no longer as an exogenous (outside) but as an endogenous (inside) element in the working of the economic system.

Part I of the *Paper* is a restatement of the argument of a book by Professors Buchanan and Wagner recently published in the USA,[1] which should be read for a fuller version of their analysis. Mr Burton's Part II offers a new approach to British pre- and post-war and more recent economic history in the light of the Buchanan/Wagner critique of Keynes. Part III suggests the consequential new approach to contemporary and future politico-economic policy.

Not the least novel and fundamental of the proposals is that a change in the constitution is required to ensure that government is prevented from pursuing its own interests at the expense of the public. Here is one of the main insights of the new economics of politics. It displaces the conventional view that government can be safely trusted to operate in the public interest by demonstrating that, on the contrary, it must be expected to be generally engaged in operating against the long-term public interest by serving its short-term political advantage.

This *Hobart Paper* was suggested by Professor Buchanan, an adviser of the Institute. It offers teachers and students of economics a provocative and stimulating new approach to the economic policy of Keynes that should begin or consolidate a new development in thinking and debate in Britain on the power of government to harm the people. It will, for that reason, be of exceptional interest to non-economists in government, industry and the media as a new explanation of Britain's economic discontents.

March 1978   ARTHUR SELDON

[1] *Democracy in Deficit, The Political Legacy of Lord Keynes*, Academic Press, New York and London, 1977.

THE AUTHORS

JAMES McGILL BUCHANAN has been University Professor of Economics and Director of the Center for Study of Public Choice at the Virginia Polytechnic Institute, Blacksburg, Virginia, since 1969. Previously he was Professor of Economics at Florida State University, 1951-56, University of Virginia (and Director of the Thomas Jefferson Center for Political Economy), 1956-68, and University of California at Los Angeles, 1968-69. He is the author of numerous works on aspects of the economics of politics and public choice, including *The Calculus of Consent* (with Gordon Tullock) (1962), *Public Finance in Democratic Process* (1967), *Demand and Supply of Public Goods* (1968), *Public Principles of Public Debt* (1958), *The Limits of Liberty: Between Anarchy and Leviathan* (1975), and (with Richard E. Wagner) *Democracy in Deficit: The Political Legacy of Lord Keynes* (1977). Professor Buchanan is a member of the IEA's Advisory Council. The IEA has published his *The Inconsistencies of the National Health Service* (Occasional Paper 7, 1965).

RICHARD E. WAGNER is Professor of Economics at Virginia Polytechnic Institute and State University. He has taught micro- and macro-economic theory, public finance, and urban economics. He is the author or co-author of several books, including *The Fiscal Organization of American Federalism* (1971), *The Public Economy* (1973), *Perspectives on Tax Reform* (1974), *Inheritance and the State* (1977), and (with Professor Buchanan) *Democracy in Deficit*. He has contributed articles to the journals of economics and public policy, and to a recent collection of essays on *Parents, Teachers and Children: Prospects for Choice in American Education* (1977).

JOHN BURTON is Principal Lecturer in Economics at Kingston Polytechnic. He was previously an economic consultant to the National Board for Prices and Incomes, the Office of Manpower Economics, and the OECD. He is the author of *Wage Inflation* (1972), and of articles in the journals. He contributed a paper, 'Are Trade Unions a Public Good/'Bad'?: The Economics of the Closed Shop', to IEA Readings No. 17, *Trade Unions: Public Goods or Public 'Bads'?* (1978).

PART I

**Democracy and Keynesian Constitutions:
Political Biases and Economic Consequences**

JAMES M. BUCHANAN and RICHARD E. WAGNER

A. VISIONS OF THE ECONOMIC ORDER: CLASSICAL AND KEYNESIAN

The Classical or pre-Keynesian notions of prudent fiscal conduct were reasonably summarised by drawing an analogy between the state and the family. It was another British intellectual 'export', Adam Smith, who noted that 'What is prudence in the conduct of every private family, can scarce be folly in that of a great kingdom'. Prudent financial conduct by the state was conceived in basically the same image as that for the family. Frugality, not profligacy, was the cardinal virtue, and this norm assumed practical shape in the widely shared principle that public budgets should be in balance, if not in surplus, and that deficits were to be tolerated only in extraordinary circumstances. Substantial and continuing deficits were interpreted as the mark of fiscal folly. Principles of sound family and business practice were deemed equally relevant to the fiscal affairs of the state.

During this period, a free-enterprise economy was generally held as being characterised by 'Say's Equality'.[1] While fluctuations in economic activity would occur in such an economy, they would set in motion self-correcting forces that would operate to restore prosperity. Within this economic framework, the best action for government was simply to avoid injecting additional sources of instability into the economy. The profligacy of government was one latent source of disturbance, and it was considered important that this governmental proclivity should be restrained. Avoiding such sources of instability, along with keeping debt and taxes low so as to promote thrift and saving, was the way to achieve prosperity. A balanced or surplus budget was one of the practical rules that reflected such constraints and beliefs. Such siren songs as the 'paradox of thrift' were yet to come.[2]

From Classical stability to Keynesian instability

The idea that the spontaneous co-ordination of economic activities within a system of markets would generally produce

[1] A recent re-statement of this perspective is in W. H. Hutt, *A Rehabilitation of Say's Law*, Ohio University Press, Athens, Ohio, 1974. 'Say's Equality' (after J. B. Say, the French 19th-century classical economist) is usually summarised as the proposition that 'supply creates its own demand', provided that markets operate in a competitive manner.

[2] The 'paradox of thrift' is the Keynesian proposition that a reduction in thriftiness (an increase in private or governmental spending propensities) will boost the economy.

[13]

economic stability was replaced in the Keynesian vision by the idea of an inherently unstable economy. Say's Equality was deemed inapplicable. The Keynesian paradigm was one of an economy alternately haunted by gluts and secular stagnation.[1] The prosperous co-ordination of economic activities was a razor's edge. The economic order is as likely to be saddled with substantial unemployment as it is to provide full employment. An important element in the Keynesian paradigm was the absence of an equilibrating process by which inconsistencies among the plans of the participants in the economic process became self-correcting. Prosperity, accordingly, could be assured only through deliberate efforts of government to help the economy avoid the buffeting forces of inflation and recession. 'Fine tuning' became the ideal of Keynesian economic policy.

The Keynesian message, in other words, contained two central features. One was the image of an inherently unstable economy, ungoverned by some 'natural law' of a generally smooth co-ordination of economic activities. The other was of government as having both the obligation and the ability to offset this instability so as to bring about a more smoothly functioning economic order. The notion of an unstable economy whose performance could be improved through the manipulation of public budgets produced a general principle that budgets *need not* be in balance: indeed, they *should not* be in balance, since that would mean government was failing in its duty. Some years of deficit and others of surplus were both necessary to, and evidence of, corrective macro-economic management. A stable relation between revenues and expenditures, say a relatively constant rate of surplus, would indicate a failure of government to carry out its managerial duties.

B. The Idealised Environment for Keynesian Economic Policy

While Lord Keynes published his *General Theory* in 1936, his presuppositions did not infuse themselves into generally held understandings or beliefs for about a generation in America,

[1] A specific discussion of these two economic cosmologies is in Axel Leijonhufvud, 'Effective Demand Failures', *Swedish Journal of Economics*, 75, March 1973, pp. 31-33.

though sooner in Britain, much as he anticipated in a famous passage on the time-lag between the articulation of an idea and its influence on policy.[1] While the Keynesian vision of the nature of our economic order and the proper pattern of budgetary policy gained dominance in academia in the 1940s and 1950s, it did not filter into the general climate of American opinion until the 1960s. With this conversion or shift in generally-held perspectives or beliefs, macro-economic engineering became the province of government.[2]

As developed by the economists who advocated macro-economic engineering, fiscal policy would be devoted to smoothing out cycles in private economic activity. Fiscal policy would be guided by the same principle during both recession and inflation. Deficits would be created during recession and surpluses during inflation, with the object of smoothing out peaks and troughs. The policy precepts of Keynesian economics were alleged to be wholly symmetrical. In depressed economic conditions, budget deficits would be required to restore full employment and prosperity. When inflation threatened, budget surpluses would be appropriate. The time-honoured norm of budget balance was thus jettisoned, but, in the pure logic Keynesian policy, there was no one-way departure. It might even be said that Keynesian economics did not destroy the principle of a balanced budget, but only lengthened the time-period over which it applied, from a calender year to the period of a business cycle. In this way, rational public policy would operate to promote a more prosperous and stable economy during both recession and inflation.

While the idealised setting for the symmetrical application of Keynesian economic policy is familiar, the political setting within which the policy is to be formulated and implemented is much less familiar. We have now learned that mere ex-

[1] 'I am sure that the power of vested interests is vastly exaggerated compared with the gradual encroachment of ideas. Not, indeed, immediately, but after a certain interval; for in the field of economic and political philosophy there are not many who are influenced by new theories after they are twenty-five or thirty years of age, so that the ideas which civil servants and politicians and even agitators apply to current events are not likely to be the newest. But, soon or late, it is ideas, not vested interests, which are dangerous for good or evil.' (J. M. Keynes, *The General Theory of Employment, Interest and Money*, Macmillan, 1936, pp. 383-84.)

[2] A thorough survey of this shift in paradigm toward fiscal policy in the United States is in Herbert Stein, *The Fiscal Revolution in America*, University of Chicago Press, Chicago, 1969.

hortations to politicians to promote prosperity do not guarantee they will do so: they may lack the knowledge required to promote such an outcome, or the incentive to act in the required manner, or both. In other words, the actions of politicians on budgetary policy as well as on other types of policy depend upon both the knowledge politicians have and the incentives they confront.

Keynes's defective assumptions

Keynes largely begged questions pertaining to knowledge. Central to his approach was the presumption that economists could possess knowledge sufficient to enable them to give advice which, if acted upon, would facilitate the co-ordination of human activities within the economic order. This extremely questionable assumption about knowledge melded nicely with his normative assumptions about political conduct. Keynes was an élitist, and he operated under what his biographer called the 'presuppositions of Harvey Road'—that governmental policy, and economic policy in particular, would be made by a relatively small group of wise and enlightened people.[1] Keynes did not consider the application of his policy prescriptions in a contemporary democratic setting—in which government is tempted to yield to group pressures to retain or return to power. Rather, the small group of enlightened men who made economic policy would, he assumed, subconsciously—even if in defiance of historical experience—always tend to act in accordance with the 'public interest', even when this might run foul of constituency, sectional or other organised pressures.

In the unreal economic and political environment envisaged by Keynes, there could be little or no question raised about the application of the Keynesian policy instruments. To secure a stable, prosperous economy, expenditures would be expanded and contracted symmetrically. Budget deficits would be created during periods of sluggish economic activity, and surpluses as the pace of economic activity became too quick. There would be no political pressures, he implicitly supposed,

---

[1] 'We have seen that he [Keynes] was strongly imbued with what I have called the presuppositions of Harvey Road. One of these presuppositions may perhaps be summarised in the idea that the government of Britain was and would continue to be in the hands of an intellectual aristocracy using the method of persuasion.' (The late Sir Roy Harrod, *The Life of John Maynard Keynes*, Macmillan, 1951, pp. 192-93.) Harvey Road was the location of the Keynes family residence in Cambridge.

operating to render the surpluses fictional and the deficits disproportionately large or ill-timed. The ruling élite would be guided by the presuppositions of Harvey Road; they would not act as competitors for electoral favour in a democratic political environment. There was little awareness that the dictates of political survival might run contrary to the requirements of macroeconomic engineering (assuming for now that the economic order is aptly described by the Keynesian paradigm). It was tacitly assumed either that the political survival of politicians was automatically strengthened as they came to follow more fully the appropriate fiscal policies, or that the ruling élite would act without regard to their political fortunes. But what happens when we make non-Keynesian assumptions about politics? What if we commence from the assumption that elected politicians respond to pressures emanating from constituents and the state bureaucracy? When this shift of perspective is made in the political setting for analysis, the possibilities that policy precepts may unleash political biases cannot be ignored. On this score, it should be noted that Keynes's own biographer seemed prescient, for in continuing his discussion of the presuppositions of Harvey Road, he mused:

'If, owing to the needs of planning, the functions of government became very far-reaching and multifarious, would it be possible for the intellectual aristocracy to remain in essential control? Keynes tended till the end to think of the really important decisions being reached by a small group of intelligent people, like the group that fashioned the Bretton Woods plan. But would not a democratic government having a wide multiplicity of duties tend to get out of control and act in a way of which the intelligent would not approve?

This is another dilemma—how to reconcile the functioning of a planning and interfering democracy with the requirement that in the last resort the best considered judgement should prevail. It may be that the presuppositions of Harvey Road were so much of a second nature to Keynes that he did not give this dilemma the full consideration which it deserves.'[1]

[1] *Ibid.*, p. 193.

c. Keynesian Presuppositions, Democratic Politics, and Economic Policy

Anyone, citizens no less than politicians, would typically like to live beyond his means. Individual citizens generally face a personal or household budget constraint which prevents them from acting on this desire, although some counterfeit and others go bankrupt. In the century before the shift in belief wrought by the Keynesian revolution, politicians acted as if they sensed a similar constraint when making the nation's budgetary choices.

Contemporary political institutions, however, are constrained differently because of the general belief in the Keynesian vision. This shift in constraints due to the shift in general beliefs alters the character of governmental budgetary policy. While there is little political resistance to budget deficits, there is substantial resistance to budget surpluses. Hence, fiscal policy will tend to be applied asymmetrically: deficits will be created frequently, but surpluses will materialise only rarely. This bias results from the shift in the general, public impression or understanding of the Western economic order, and of the related rules of thumb held generally by the citizenry as to what constitutes prudent, reasonable, or efficacious conduct by government in running its budget. Old-fashioned beliefs about the virtue of the balanced-budget rule and of redeeming public debt during periods of prosperity became undermined by Keynesian ideas, and lost their hold upon the public. In consequence, debt reduction lost its claim as a guiding rule. Budget surpluses lost their *raison d'être*. Deficits allow politicians to increase spending without having directly and openly to raise taxes. There is little obstacle to such a policy. Surpluses, on the other hand, require government to raise taxes without increasing spending—a programme far more capable of stimulating political opposition than budget deficits, especially once the constraining norm of debt retirement had receded from public consciousness.

Market and political competition: similarities and essential differences

In a democracy, political competition bears certain resemblances to market competition. Private firms compete among themselves in numerous, complex ways to secure the patronage of customers. Politicians compete among themselves for the support of the electorate by offering and promising policies and programmes which they hope will get them elected or re-elected. A politician in a democratic society, in other words, can be viewed as proposing and attempting to enact a combination of expenditure programmes and financing schemes that will secure him the support of a majority of the electorate. This realistic view of the formulation of economic policy in a political democracy found no place in Keynes's *General Theory*. Its absence made his policy proposals unsound, because unrealistic.

There are also, it is worth noting, important differences between market and political competition. Market competition is continuous; at each purchase, a buyer is able to select among competing sellers. Political competition is intermittent; a decision is binding generally (as in the USA) for a fixed number of years. Market competition allows several competitors to survive simultaneously; the capture by one seller of a majority of the market does not deny the ability of the minority to choose their preferred supplier. Political competition leads to an all-or-nothing outcome: the capture of a majority of a market gives the entire market to that supplier. Again, in market competition, the buyer can be reasonably certain as to just what it is that he will receive from his purchase. In political competition, the buyer is in effect purchasing the services of an agent, whom he cannot bind in matters of specific compliance, and to whom he is forced to grant wide latitude in the use of discretionary judgement. Politicians are simply not held liable for their promises and pledges as are private sellers. Moreover, because a politician needs to secure the co-operation of a majority of politicians, the meaning of a vote for a politician is less clear than that of a 'vote' for a private firm. For these reasons, among others, political competition is different from, and inferior to, market competition, even though there is a fundamental similarity.[1] This was generally overlooked in economic analysis until recent years, and entirely ignored by Keynes and the Keynesians who followed him.

Budgets: political gains and losses

The essential feature of democratic budgetary choice may be illustrated by considering the gains and losses to politicians of

[1] A fuller examination of the similarities and differences is in James M. Buchanan, 'Individual Choice in Voting and the Market', *Journal of Political Economy*, 62, August 1954, pp. 334-43; reprinted in *idem, Fiscal Theory and Political Economy*, University of North Carolina Press, Chapel Hill, 1960, pp. 90-104.

supporting various-sized budgets, and the taxes and expenditures they entail. It is the expectation of political gains and losses from alternative taxing and spending programmes which shapes the budgetary outcomes that emerge within a democratic system of political competition. The size and composition of public budgets in such a system of competitive democracy can thus be viewed as a result of the preferences of a politician's constituents and the constitutional-institutional rules that constrain the political system.

With a balanced-budget rule, any proposal for expenditure must be coupled with a proposal for taxation. The elimination of the balanced-budget rule as a result of the advent of the Keynesian revolution altered the institutional constraints within which democratic politics operates. The nature of the pressures of political competition consequently would differ in this revised, Keynesian constitutional setting from what they were in the Classical constitutional setting. What we must do now is consider the respective survival prospects of budget surpluses and budget deficits, showing in the process that deficits have stronger political survival value than surpluses once the Keynesian vision and its concomitant beliefs replaced the Classical vision.

(i) Budget surpluses and democratic politics

Assuming an initial situation of budget balance, the creation of a budget surplus requires an increase in real rates of tax, a decrease in real rates of public spending, or some combination of the two. In any event, budget surpluses will impose direct and immediate costs on some or all of the citizenry. If taxes are increased, some persons will have their disposable incomes reduced. If public spending is reduced, some beneficiaries of public services will suffer. In terms of *direct* consequences, a policy of budget surpluses will create losers among the citizenry, but no gainers.

Gainers must be sought for in the *indirect* consequences of budget surpluses. There may be some general acceptance of the notion that the prevention of inflation is a desirable objective for national economic policy. It could be argued that people should be able to see beyond the direct consequences of budget surpluses to the *indirect* consequences. They should understand that a budget surplus was required to prevent inflation, and that this was beneficial. The dissipation of a surplus through public spending or tax cuts, therefore, would not be costless, for it would destroy the benefits that would result from the control of inflation.

These direct and indirect consequences act quite differently on the choices of typical citizens. The direct consequences of the surplus take the form of reductions in *presently enjoyed consumption*. If taxes are raised, the consumption of private services is reduced. If government spending is lowered, the consumption of government services is reduced. In either case, a budget surplus requires citizens to sacrifice services they are consuming.

The indirect consequences, on the other hand, are of an altogether different nature. The benefit side of a budget surplus is not directly experienced, but rather must be *imagined*. It takes the form of the hypothetical or imagined gains from *avoiding* what would otherwise have been an inflationary experience.[1]

A variety of evidence suggests that these two types of choices are psychologically quite different. Moreover, appreciation of the benefits from a budget surplus would require a good deal of information and understanding. The task is not a simple matter of choosing whether to bear $100 more in taxes this year in exchange for $120 of benefits in two years, and then somehow comparing the two, historically distinct, situations. The imagining process requires an additional step. The person must form some judgement of how he, *personally*, will be affected by the surplus; he must reduce his estimate of the total ('macroeconomic') impact of the surplus to a personal ('microeconomic') level. As such future gains become more remote and less subject to personal control, however, there is strong evidence to suggest that such future circumstances tend to be neglected. 'Out of sight, out of mind' is the commonsense statement of this effect.[2]

[1] This point about the categorical difference between present and future has been a theme of many of the writings of G. L. S. Shackle. A terse statement appears in his *Epistemics and Economics,* Cambridge University Press, 1972, p. 245: 'We cannot have experience of actuality at two distinct "moments". The moment of actuality, the moment in being, "the present", is *solitary.* Extended time, beyond "the moment", appears in this light as a figment, a product of thought' (Shackle's italics).

[2] And even to the extent that citizens do creatively imagine such alternative, conjectural futures, democratic budgetary processes may produce a different form of bias against the surplus. To the extent that budgetary institutions permit fragmented appropriations, for instance, a 'prisoner's dilemma' (in which choices made by each person individually will produce undesirable
[*Continued on page 22*]

Budget surpluses clearly have weaker survival prospects in a political democracy than in a social order controlled by a set of Keynesian wise men following the presuppositions of Harvey Road. Budget surpluses may emerge in a democratic political system, but democratic political processes possess institutional biases against them. Viewed in this light, there really should be no difficulty in understanding why we have never observed the explicit creation of budget surpluses during the post-Keynesian years.

(ii) *Budget deficits and democratic politics*

In a democratic society, there would be no obstacles to budget deficits in a Keynesian economic setting. Budget deficits make it possible to spend without taxing. Whether the deficit is created through reduced taxes or increased expenditures, the form each takes will, of course, determine the distribution of gains among citizens. The key difference from a budget surplus, however, is that there are only direct gainers from such deficits and no losers.

Deficits will also create losers indirectly, due to the resulting inflation. Such indirect consequences are, however, dimensionally different, as we have seen. The direct consequences of debt creation take the form of increased consumption of currently enjoyed services; these would be privately-provided services if the deficit took place through a tax reduction, and government-provided services if through an increase in government expenditure. The indirect consequences, however, relate not to present experience, but to future conjecture. The benefit of deficit finance resides in the increase in currently enjoyed services, whereas the cost resides in the inflationary impact upon the future, in the creatively-imagined reduction in well-being at some future date. The analysis of these indirect con-

[*Continued from page 21*]
results compared with what would result if all made a common choice) will tend to operate to dissipate revenues that might produce a budget surplus. Suppose, for instance, that a potential $10 billion budget surplus is prevented from arising due to the presentation of 10 separate spending proposals of $1 billion each, as opposed to the presentation of a single expenditure proposal of $10 billion. In the first case, although each participant may recognise that he would be better off if none of the spending proposals carry, institutions that allow separate, fragmented budgetary consideration may operate to create a result that is mutually undesirable, akin to the prisoner's dilemma. An analysis of this possibility is in James M. Buchanan and Gordon Tullock, *The Calculus of Consent*, University of Michigan Press, Ann Arbor, 1962, especially Ch. 10.

sequences is essentially the same as that of the indirect consequences of the budget surplus.

A democratic society, therefore, will tend to resort to an excessive use of deficit finance once acceptance of the Keynesian paradigm has led to a revision of the fiscal constitution. For this reason, the post-Keynesian record in fiscal policy is not difficult to understand. The removal of the balanced-budget principle of constitutional rule generated an asymmetry in the conduct of budgetary policy in our form of competitive democracy. Deficits are created, but to a larger extent than justified by the Keynesian principles; surpluses sometimes result, but they occur less frequently than required by Keynesian prescriptions. When plausible assumptions are made about the institutions of decision-making in political democracy, the effect is to increase the biases against the use of budgetary adjustments to prevent and control inflation, as well as to increase the bias toward budgetary adjustments aimed at stimulating spending.

(iii) Keynesian economics in political democracy

The grafting of Keynesian economics onto the fabric of a political democracy has wrought a significant revision in the underlying fiscal constitution. The result has been a tendency toward budget deficits and, consequently, once the workings of democratic political institutions are taken into account, inflation. Democratic governments will generally respond more vigorously in correcting for unemployment than in correcting for inflation. Budgetary adjustments aimed at the prevention or control of inflation will rarely be observed as the result of deliberate policy. Budget deficits will come to be the general rule, even when inflation is severe. In slack years, when deficits might seem warranted by strict application of the Keynesian precepts, the size of these deficits will become disproportionately large. Moreover, the perceived cost of government will generally be lower than the real cost because of the deficit financing. As a consequence, there will also be a relative increase in the size of the government sector in the economy. Budget deficits, inflation, and the growth of government—all are intensified by the Keynesian destruction of former constitutional principles of sound finance.

D. The Destructive, Self-fulfilling Character of the Keynesian Political Biases

These political biases towards budget deficits also become a bias towards inflation, because monetary institutions as they are currently constituted operate, to some extent, to increase the stock of money in response to budget deficits. The one-sided application of Keynesian policy precepts which emerges from a democratic political setting may itself create economic instability in the process.

While inflation is usually thought of as a *proportionate* rise in all prices, as a rise in the absolute level of prices, in practice the structure of *relative* prices changes as well.[1] Indeed, what are commonly referred to as macro-economic policies are not instruments intended to influence all prices proportionately, but rather are instruments intended to influence the structure of *relative* prices. The dictates of political survival operate in this direction because it is only through policies designed to act on relative prices that the vote-buying activities of politicians and parties can take place. A macro-economic policy aimed only at the general price level would be typified by an indiscriminate dropping of money from a helicopter.[2] But any such non-discriminatory policy would be defeated politically by a policy designed to benefit specific recipients, such as a spending programme in marginal constituencies. In other words, the primary phenomenon to be considered in examining the inflationary bias of Keynesian economics is not the level of absolute prices, but rather the change in the structure of relative prices. Macro-economic consequences are simply the sum of these micro-economic consequences.[3]

Once it is recognised that the important consequence of inflation is its impact on relative prices, and particularly once it is recognised that rational political action would aim at selective shifts in relative prices rather than at non-selective shifts in absolute prices, a new perspective on the destructive

---

[1] Discussed, for instance, by Daniel R. Vining and Thomas C. Elwertowski, 'The Relationship between Relative Prices and the General Price Level', *American Economic Review*, 66, September 1976, pp. 699-708.

[2] A popular, textbook abstraction of the nature of macro-economic policy originated by Professor Don Patinkin.

[3] For example, Friedrich A. Hayek, *Monetary Theory and the Trade Cycle*, Harcourt Brace, New York, 1932; and *idem*, *Prices and Production*, 2nd Edn., Routledge and Kegan Paul, 1935.

character of the Keynesian political biases emerges.[1] This is particularly true once it is also recognised that the essential nature of the economic order is vastly different from that implied by the standard treatments of inflation and macro-economic policy. In these standard treatments the economy is viewed much like a balloon. Blow and the economy expands; suck and it contracts. This vision of the economy inherent in most macro-economic models makes it appear to be a simple matter to achieve both the desired *degree* of inflation or contraction and the desired *timing* of those expansions and contractions.

Such a view of the economic order, while making life easy for economists, hardly conforms to economic experience. Rather, an economy is a complex web of contractual relations that reflect the anticipations and plans of the various participants. Metaphorically, it is far more like a gigantic erector set running throughout a 200-room mansion, with each piece connected to pieces in many different rooms. Changes made at one point will exert effects throughout the system, and will do so with varying time delays. *And no one person will be able to apprehend the entire apparatus*, quite unlike the case of the balloon. Moreover, shifts taking place at one point can be the consequence of earlier shifts elsewhere, and there is no assurance about the consequences of additional changes made at that point.

Today's economic occurrences and disturbances are a complex, only partially-apprehendable result of previous changes in many places at many different times in the past. Thus, the injection of new changes in budgetary policy is quite unlike inflating or deflating a balloon.[2] It is rather like readjusting some of the particular links in the erector set, only the metaphor should be even more complicated because the individual nodes have a will, so, therefore, they can think, create, and act.[3]

---

[1] Much of this is discussed in Richard E. Wagner, 'Economic Manipulation for Political Profit: Macroeconomic Consequences and Constitutional Implications', *Kyklos*, 30, No. 3, 1977, pp. 395-410.

[2] Further discussion of the neglect of the real world of complex micro-relations in orthodox macro-economic analysis is in L. M. Lachmann, *Macro-economic Thinking and the Market Economy*, Hobart Paper 56, IEA, 1973.

[3] See particularly such works by Henri Bergson as *Essai sur les données immédiates de la conscience*, F. Alcan, Paris, 1899; and idem, *L'Evolution créatrice*, F. Alcan, Paris, 1907. A related treatment within the context of economic analysis is in G. L. S. Shackle, *Decision, Order, and Time in Human Affairs*, Cambridge University Press, 1961.

These readjustments will disturb a whole set of anticipations and plans, with the consequences of these readjustments extending over various periods.

Hayek's analysis of the impact of inflation

There are several facets to the story about how the shifts in relative prices, induced by inflation, can have disco-ordinating impacts upon our economic order. One was articulated by Professor F. A. Hayek in the 1930s.[1] The initial impact of the inflation in Hayek's analysis was to shift the structure of relative prices in favour of capital goods of long gestation periods. The resultant lengthening of the structure of production, however, is inconsistent with the underlying data of wants, resources and knowledge. Such a pattern of employment and output cannot be maintained without an acceleration of the inflation. But a continually accelerating inflation is not sustainable as a long-run feature of an economic order. In the absence of such acceleration, the structure of production will revert to its former state. This process of readjustment leads to unemployment and recession. A recession becomes a necessary price of the *political* activities that produced the inflation in the first place, unless some movement toward an incomes policy to repress the inflation takes place, in which event the distortions would simply manifest themselves somewhat differently. Reallocations of labour must take place before the economy's structure of production will once again reflect the underlying data to which the economy adapts. Thus people respond to non-sustainable price signals generated by the inflation and the resulting mistakes must be worked out before the economy can return to normalcy. Recession is an inherent part of the recovery process.

In Hayek's framework, the excessive expansion occurred in the capital goods industries. In these days of massive government spending, however, the story is more complex, for it is the activities on which politicians increase spending that generate an excessive absorption of resources. This attraction of resources due to the shift in relative prices need not be confined to the capital goods industries, because there can be other industries that will be differentially favoured by the government spending policies. Nonetheless, the central consequence remains: a pattern of resource allocation will be brought about

[1] *Prices and Production*, Routledge & Kegan Paul, 1931.

[26]

that is not sustainable without still further efforts at distorting the structure of relative prices through inflationary finance. The Keynesian inflationary biases can be considerably more destructive than a simple increase in the general price level, because the changes in relative prices lead to further distortions as people act on the basis of price signals that are inconsistent with the underlying structure of preferences and technology. As a result of these mistakes, decisions will be made on investment and the employment of resources that are not sustainable by the economy. Unemployment and capital waste will then result as people readjust their plans and actions to correct mistakes based on erroneous signals in the economy.

e. Conclusion

Why does Camelot[1] lie in ruins? Intellectual error of monumental proportion has been made, and not exclusively by the politicians. Error also lies squarely with the economists. The 'academic scribbler' who must bear substantial responsibility is Lord Keynes, whose thinking was uncritically accepted by establishment economists in both America and Britain. The mounting historical evidence of the ill-effects of Keynes's ideas cannot continue to be ignored. Keynesian economics has turned the politicians loose; it has destroyed the effective constraint on politicians' ordinary appetites to spend and spend without the apparent necessity to tax.

Sober assessment suggests that, politically, Keynesianism represents a substantial disease that over the long run can prove fatal for the survival of democracy.

---

[1] [Camelot was the capital of King Arthur's ideal society of chivalric literature from the 10th to the 13th centuries. It proved unfeasible because good intentions belied human nature.—ED.]

PART II

Keynes's Legacy to Great Britain: 'Folly in a Great Kingdom'

JOHN BURTON

ACKNOWLEDGEMENTS

I am grateful to Dr M. Hawkins and Dr I. Hannaford of King-ston Polytechnic for their comments on the political and constitutional aspects of this Section; and to Ralph Harris and Arthur Seldon for their painstaking workover, probing criticism and stimulating suggestions on an earlier draft.

March 1978

J.B.

A. Britain's Changing Fiscal History

In 1790 the total expenditure of the public authorities in Britain stood at £23 million in money terms, and accounted for approximately 12 per cent of gross national product (GNP). Although government expenditure was to rise substantially in both money and real terms over the ensuing century, in 1913 government expenditure accounted for the same fraction of GNP as it did in 1790—12 per cent. Today, the picture is somewhat different. An official document records its broad features, as it has evolved over recent years, in terse terms:

'In the last three years public expenditure has grown nearly 20 per cent in volume, while output has risen less than two per cent. The ratio of public expenditure to gross domestic product at factor cost has risen from 50 per cent in 1971-2 to about 60 per cent in 1975-6.'[1]

What explains this vast transformation in the size, significance and growth of the British budgetary accounts?

The pre-Keynesian budgetary record

Table I records the behaviour and significance of government expenditure in Britain for selected years before the Keynesian revolution in economic thought and policy. These figures reveal the same general time-pattern as those relating to the pre-Keynesian budgetary record of the USA, discussed in *Democracy in Deficit*.[2] Public expenditure tended to rise at times of international conflict—the Napoleonic Wars (1793-1815), the Crimean War (1854-56), the Zulu Wars (1880), the Boer War (1899-1902), and the First World War (1914-18)—and also during periods of economic recession, such as the inter-war depression of the 1930s. The emergence of budget deficits was similarly and generally confined to periods of war—the major instance being that of the First World War—and of economic setback. In 'normal' years, when peace and prosperity reigned, governments aimed for a balance between their expenditure and revenue, if not for a small budget surplus, so that something was available to reduce the borrowings run up during preceding war periods. As Table I shows, the National Debt therefore showed a tendency to fall in the 'normal' years.

---

[1] Information Division of HM Treasury, *Economic Progress Report,* No. 72, March 1976, p. 2.

[2] *Op. cit.*

[31]

TABLE I

THE PRE-KEYNESIAN BRITISH BUDGETARY RECORD,
Selected Years, 1790-1935

	(i) Total Government Expenditure (at current prices, rounded to nearest £1 million)	(ii) Government Expenditure as a percentage of Gross National Product	(iii) Rise (+) or Fall (–) in National Debt (£ million in nominal terms)
1790	23	12	n.a.*
1800	67	22	n.a.
1814	123	29	n.a.
1820	70	17	n.a.
1830	65	15	n.a.
1840	64	11	+4**
1850	64	11	–4
1860	87	11	–1
1870	92	9	–5
1880	112	10	–6
1890	131	9	–6
1895	157	10	–9
1900	281	14	+62
1905	242	12	–12
1910	272	13	–28
1913	305	12	–10
1918	2,427	52	+1,563
1920	1,592	26	–255
1925	1,072	24	–39
1932	1,138	29	+210
1935	1,117	24	–4

* n.a.=not available

** =1841 figure

Sources: Columns (i) and (ii): 1790-1880 figures taken from J. Ververka, 'The Growth of Government Expenditure in the United Kingdom since 1790', *Scottish Journal of Political Economy*, Vol. 10, 1967; 1890-1935 figures taken from A. T. Peacock and J. Wiseman, *The Growth of Public Expenditure in the United Kingdom*, Oxford University Press, 1961, Table A-5, pp. 164-5. Column (iii): I am grateful to Mr D. J. Reid of the Central Statistical Office for providing me with a series on the National Debt extending back into the 19th century.

The Keynesian budgetary record

In the Second World War, Keynes—by then the most eminent and famous economist of his generation—entered the British Treasury as a 'demi-semi-official' (as he described his position). This post, his public stature, and the vast system of contacts with establishment figures that Keynes had acquired over the years, were to place him in a position of powerful influence. The 1941 budget was the first to be constructed on the principles of Keynesian macro-management ideas, which became the Treasury orthodoxy.[1]

Furthermore, in this triumphant return to the corridors of power, Keynes had been accompanied by a retinue of younger disciples such as James Meade and Richard Stone. These disciples, and particularly Meade, were to provide much of the impetus towards the further implementation of a Keynesian régime. From this intellectual milieu and bureaucratic power-base emerged such famous milestones in British public policy as the 1942 Beveridge Report, and the 1944 White Papers on *Employment Policy* and *Social Insurance*. The year 1944 thus marks the birth of the Keynesian revolution in UK governmental policy. Since that time, Britain has had a Keynesian fiscal constitution: that is, there has been no constitutional restraint on governments to prevent them from running a budget deficit.

Some aspects of the British experience with this new fiscal constitution are shown in Table II. Government expenditure—both in nominal terms and as a proportion of national output—has grown secularly at an unprecedented rate. Furthermore, this has been a period during which Britain has not been involved in any major international conflicts (with the exception of the Korean War, 1950-51), and which also has been generally characterised by boom conditions in the world (and British) economy from the late 'forties until 1974.

The secular behaviour and significance of the budget deficit is also now clearly different from that in the pre-Keynesian era. Budget deficits under the new fiscal constitution, in comparison to the 'normal' years of the 19th century, have become vast and persistent. Only in a few post-war years (such as 1969-70) has

[1] A detailed account of the Keynesian colonisation of the Treasury and the Economic Section of the Cabinet Secretariat during the war is in D. E. Moggridge, 'Economic Policy in the Second World War', in M. Keynes (ed.), *Essays on John Maynard Keynes*, Cambridge University Press, 1975.

TABLE II
THE KEYNESIAN BRITISH BUDGETARY RECORD:
Annual Figures, 1946-76

	Total Public Expenditure (£m., current prices)	Public Expenditure as a % of GDP at factor cost	Budget Deficit (−) or Surplus (+) £m., current prices)*	Budget Deficit as a percentage of GDP at factor cost**	Deficit-Financed Public Expenditure as a % of percentage Total Public Expenditure
1946	4,582	52·05	n.a.	n.a.	n.a.
1947	4,327	46·32	n.a.	n.a.	n.a.
1948	4,577	44·65	n.a.	n.a.	n.a.
1949	4,816	43·77	n.a.	n.a.	n.a.
1950	4,881	42·88	n.a.	n.a.	n.a.
1951	5,752	45·59	n.a.	n.a.	n.a.
1952	6,455	46·91	− 771	5·60	11·94
1953	6,750	46·13	− 591	4·04	8·76
1954	6,641	42·63	− 367	2·36	5·53
1955	7,048	41·88	− 469	2·79	6·65
1956	7,495	41·54	− 564	3·13	7·53
1957	7,903	41·57	− 486	2·56	6·15
1958	8,269	41·72	− 491	2·48	5·94
1959	8,769	41·87	− 571	2·73	6·51
1960	9,398	41·26	− 710	3·12	7·55
1961	10,319	42·83	− 704	2·92	6·82
1962	11,013	43·70	− 546	2·17	4·96
1963	11,657	43·41	− 842	3·16	7·22
1964	12,759	43·92	− 989	3·40	7·75
1965	14,137	45·28	− 1,205	3·86	8·52
1966	15,317	46·46	− 961	2·92	6·27
1967	17,520	50·66	− 1,863	5·39	10·63
1968	19,106	51·30	− 1,278	3·43	6·69
1969	19,778	49·95	+ 466 (−)	1·18	—
1970	21,866	50·17	+ 17 (−)	0·04	—
1971	24,327	49·96	− 1,372	2·82	5·64
1972	27,375	49·46	− 2,047	4·00	7·48
1973	32,316	50·69	− 4,168	6·54	12·90
1974	41,930	56·94	− 6,336	8·60	15·11
1975	54,465	59·06	−10,515	11·40	19·31
1976	58,181	53·99	− 9,512	8·83	16·35

* Income data base for GDP. **The Budget Deficit is here defined as the total public sector borrowing requirement with sign reversed. n.a.=not available.
Sources: Data drawn from *Economic Trends*, various years. I am grateful to Mr R. Arrundale of the Central Statistical Office for supplying me with previously unpublished figures on public expenditure (1946-54).

[34]

a surplus ever been encountered. In the 1970s, the public sector borrowing requirement mounted steadily to historically unprecedented levels, accounting for some 11.4 per cent of gross domestic product in 1975.

The displacement hypothesis

One explanation of the different volumes of government expenditure before and after World War II is known as the 'displacement hypothesis'. In a study of British public expenditure from 1890, Professors A. T. Peacock and J. Wiseman concluded that the growth of government expenditure occurred in a discontinuous fashion.[1] Their hypothesis was that in peacetime there is a widely-shared view of what constitutes a 'tolerable' amount of taxation, which changes only slowly over time (if at all), and sets a constraint on the volume of government expenditure. But in war, governments are forced to exceed the tax level established during the preceding peace. Old notions of what is tolerable are discarded whilst the war also generates stronger feelings of fraternity and community, and a heightened recognition of social problems. The result is that in the post-war period the 'tolerable' level of taxation, and voter demands for collective provision and financing of goods and welfare services, are both permanently 'displaced' upwards.

The displacement hypothesis at first sight appears to be a plausible theory which fits the broad facts of growth in British government expenditure. A closer inspection suggests some doubts.[2]

First, the hypothesis fails to explain the record of government expenditure during the 19th century. Table I shows no permanent upward displacements in government expenditure as a proportion of GNP, despite numerous wars. After them, public expenditure tended to return to a lower level.

Second, the displacement hypothesis fails to account for Britain's post-World War II record growth of government spending. It did not settle down to a higher level. It has grown *almost continuously* over the last three decades, at a secularly

[1] *The Growth of Public Expenditure in the United Kingdom*, Oxford University Press, 1961.

[2] It should be noted that Professors Peacock and Wiseman never intended their hypothesis to be a comprehensive explanation of the historical record of the growth of government expenditure in Britain, although that interpretation has been commonly and erroneously put on their work. The points made here seek only to clarify why it cannot be a complete explanation.

faster rate than the rate of growth of national output and the rate of growth of tax revenue.

Third, the Peacock-Wiseman analysis contains an assumption that is at variance with the reality of the post-World War II situation: that the electorally-tolerable level of tax revenue sets an upper bound on the level of government expenditure. This is certainly true of a democracy whose fiscal constitution embodies a balanced-budget rule, as broadly typified the 19th century. But it is not true of a democracy with a Keynesian fiscal constitution, as has existed since 1944. It is then possible for governments to spend, by recourse to deficit finance, more than the electorally-tolerable volume of taxation. Tax revenue no longer acts as a constraint on the level of government expenditure.

The Peacock-Wiseman analysis thus does not explain satisfactorily the long-run trends of British public expenditure in a number of ways. It is the thesis of this *Paper* that to account for the observed historical transformation from long-run stability in the share of government in GNP and peace-time balanced budgets to ever-growing government spending combined with persistent deficit finance, a further fundamental element needs to be brought into the picture: the transmogrification of Britain's fiscal constitution, during World War II, by the Keynesian revolution.

B. The Pre-Keynesian British Fiscal Constitution

The 'fiscal constitution' of any country comprises the set of constitutional rules which regulates government decisions on expenditure and finance. It is thus a major and fundamental component of the country's political constitution *in toto*. Certainly, in Britain it has been this fiscal component which has historically been the primary source of constitutional controversy and reform. The control of the public finances was the basic bone of contention between Crown and Parliament for centuries. The establishment of Parliament's right to vote the funds of government was the principal means by which it gradually gained the ascendancy as the centre of political power and gravity over the Crown. The control of public monies was also to be the crucial issue in the most serious constitutional crisis of 20th-century Britain, following which the House of Commons was to 'tame' the House of Lords *via* the Parliament Act of 1911.

[36]

Britain is almost unique amongst constitutional democracies —and indeed, amongst all modern states, democratic or otherwise—in having no written constitution and, therefore, no written fiscal constitution. The British constitution rests on a number of constitutional *conventions* that have evolved from the hard practical experience of many centuries of democratic life. The authority of these conventions thus rests on the forces of custom and acceptance alone, but 'while in force are . . . binding on rulers and ruled alike'.[1] The majority of these conventions have never been formally codified.

What were the constitutional conventions that defined the rules of fiscal behaviour in 19th-century Britain?

The conventions of the fiscal constitution in 19th-century Britain

Without a written record of official regulations, it is not easy to summarise the rules definitively. In the absence of binding written regulations, it was, furthermore, possible for constitutional rules to undergo a process of continuous, slow evolution. The British fiscal constitution in 1890 was thus not the same animal as in 1810. It is nevertheless possible to summarise the main features of 'the' 19th-century British fiscal constitution as follows:

(1) 'On common subjects any Member [of the House of Commons] can propose anything, but not on money—the Minister [Government] only can propose to tax the people [or spend money]'.[2] This convention originated in the early 18th century, and *is* codified in Standing Order No. 82 of the House of Commons.[3]

(2) The spending of public money, and the imposition of taxation, are the prerogative of Parliament as a whole, not of the Crown or the Government.

(3) Questions of government expenditure and finance are in the final analysis the prerogative of the House of Commons, not the House of Lords. This convention was implicitly observed from 1671, and finally clarified by the Parliament Act of 1911.

[1] K. Lowenstein, *British Cabinet Government*, Oxford University Press, 1964, p. 118; also W. Ivor Jennings, *The British Constitution*, Cambridge University Press, 1961.

[2] Walter Bagehot, *The English Constitution*, 1867.

[3] It stipulates that: 'This House will receive no petition for any sum relating to public service or proceed upon any motion for a grant . . . unless recommended from the Crown.' (*Standing Orders of the House of Commons*, 1969, p. 64.)

(4) All grantings of public funds, and any imposition of new taxation, must be passed in a majority vote of the House of Commons, and incorporated in an Act of Parliament.

(5) The Government's spending plans for the forthcoming fiscal year are to be presented to the House of Commons for debate in the form of a Budget Statement in the month of April. This convention was established in the Budget of 1861, and later reinforced by the reforms associated with the Expenditure and Audit Department Act of 1866.

(6) 'Redress of grievance before supply.' This archaic phrase signifies that the House of Commons will not grant any public funds to cover the Government's spending plans as announced in the Budget Statement unless and until there has been a public airing and debate upon its grievances beforehand. In practice, this meant and means today that there is an opportunity for wide-ranging debates on all sorts of motions to approve the Estimates (of government spending plans for the fiscal year) to take place. Without this convention of 'redress of grievance before supply', the House would have no power over the Government to permit the parliamentary time for such debates.

(7) The Balanced-Budget Convention. In the 19th century it became the established convention that the government should always seek to cover its planned expenditure with adequate tax (and other) revenues, if not to achieve a surplus of taxation over expenditure, in order to contribute to the reduction of the National Debt. This convention was relaxed in times of war, during which it was felt that the exigencies of the situation might require some recourse to deficit finance.[1] In ordinary times, to finance government expenditure by borrowing was in Bagehot's phrase 'shameful', and warranted public censure and castigation of a reprehensible Executive.

How well did these main planks of the British 19th-century fiscal constitution fit together?

---

[1] Ricardo argued that taxation was superior to debt creation as a means of public finance, even in war-time. The possibility of deficit finance under such circumstances, he argued, might encourage kings and governments to indulge in such military adventures in the first place.

The cohesion and functioning of the British 19th-century fiscal constitution

Discussions of British constitutional history have tended to give insufficient attention to the interaction of the foregoing fiscal-constitutional conventions.[1] In particular, it has been insufficiently recognised that, *alone*, the first six conventions (above) were a very weak reed against the predictable tendencies of a system of party-organised competitive (democratic) politics towards persistent deficit finance and government spending growth. The balanced-budget convention (rule (7)) was *absolutely crucial* to the complex of fiscal conventions in providing a constitutional check against these tendencies, and in the task of allowing the whole system of fiscal-constitutional rules to function together effectively.

This role needs to be seen against the background of a changed relationship between Crown and Government in the 19th century, and the rise of political parties in the 18th and 19th centuries. Parties (in the sense of alliances of MPs aimed at securing and retaining the spoils of office) existed in the early 18th century. These were often temporary and shifting, however, and not politically permanent alliances organised into strict voting blocs in the Commons. However, after being turned out of office by the King in 1770, the Whigs began to organise themselves into a political party in a more contemporary form. The age of party politics had emerged—at least in embryonic form.[2] Edmund Burke, in his *Observations . . . on the Present State of the Nation* (1770) noted that 'party divisions . . . are [now] inseparable from Government'. Furthermore, by the time of the Reform Act of 1832, the Crown had to accept the leadership of the majority party in the Commons as the Government of the country.

Thus, in the 19th century, as the result of these two developments, the Government was no longer responsible to the Crown (except in a symbolic sense) for its conduct, but rather to the House of Commons—theoretically, at least. As the Government had a working majority in the House organised in a permanent voting coalition, it exercised control over the House, rather than the other way about.

---

[1] For example, Sir Ivor Jennings, *op. cit.*, and K. Lowenstein, *op. cit.*

[2] Up to 1867 parties were still loose and shifting coalitions. Modern political parties are a 20th-century phenomenon (the first was the Labour Party).

[39]

The consequence was that many of Britain's fiscal-constitutional conventions were, in reality, completely ineffective as checks upon excessive expenditure or excessive resort to deficit finance by the Government. Convention (1) had been evolved to prevent MPs from voting monies to themselves or to their supporters. Rule (2) was established—only after centuries of struggle with the Crown—in order to impose a similar check on the Crown, and its appointed instrument, the Government. Once the Executive was no longer responsible to, or appointed by, the Crown, and had come to control the majority voting bloc in the Commons, rule (2) thus became an essentially symbolic constraint on the Executive's fiscal behaviour; likewise with rule (4). Furthermore, the establishment of convention (3) had earlier removed any possible check that the second chamber might impose on the budgetary malpractices of the Government sitting in the first chamber.

The conjunction of conventions (5) and (6) added a further strong bias in the British fiscal constitution towards deficit finance and excessive public expenditure. Taken together, they led to a situation whereby the Government's spending plans (the Budget) were debated and voted on (in April), long before the voting on the Government's revenue estimates and proposals, which were deferred for final approval until July.[1] The interaction of these two fiscal-constitutional conventions thus led to a situation whereby *'to itself, to Parliament and to the public the government must present its spending decisions in advance of, and in isolation from, its decisions on revenue'*.[2] Thus the interaction of these two seemingly innocuous fiscal conventions—'arrangements which in themselves hardly rise above the level of procedural habit and convenience'[3]—strongly reinforced the implicit bias of the British 19th-century fiscal constitution towards excessive government expenditure and deficit finance.

Convention (7), the balanced-budget rule, thus performed a crucial function. The other conventions, (1) to (6), had been evolved to check the fiscal behaviour of political decision-makers in the context of an earlier and very different politico-

---

[1] In order for this to occur it was (and remains) necessary for the Commons to pass a Consolidated Fund Act in March, which allows the Government enough funds 'on account' to see it through to the summer.

[2] J. Enoch Powell, 'Plan to Spend First; Find the Money Later', *Lloyds Bank Review*, April 1959, p. 22 (italics in original).

[3] *Ibid.*, p. 22.

institutional framework. Faced with the increasing strength of competitive party politics and a government-dominated Commons, these rules were completely useless as a check on excessive expenditure and deficit finance and, indeed, created a bias towards excess. The crucial function of rule (7) was thus to hold the line against this implicit bias. Without that fiscal-constitutional rule, 19th-century Britain would have experienced precisely the same fiscal trends and tendencies as it has in the post-war period—a régime of persistent deficit finance and an ever-rising level of government expenditure.

The establishment of the balanced-budget rule in 19th-century Britain

The concept and introduction of a balanced-budget rule to Britain's fiscal constitution was a product of 19th-century constitutional innovation, designed to tackle the implicit biases of the evolving political system. The background and history of that innovation and its establishment presents remarkable and fascinating comparisons with the situation of Britain today, in two main ways.

First, in the 18th century, as in Britain today, government expenditure had got out of control. From the reign of Queen Anne (1702-15) until the 1780s, the House of Commons 'made no effective attempt to enforce the responsibility of the Executive for efficient, economical government'.[1] For example, the government of Sir Robert Walpole, First Lord of the Treasury —and the *de facto* first British Prime Minister (1721-42)—has been adequately described by the phrase 'government by corruption'. Walpole wielded Crown patronage and other levers of manipulation to influence individual MPs and the aristocratic groups that controlled the nomination of parliamentary candidates:

> 'Gifts, sinecures, pensions, lucrative government contracts, unadorned bribery—they were all used. In the House of Lords, which then had just over 200 members, the distribution of titles performed the same service. Independent members of Parliament, which meant members not beholden in any way to the Government, were an exception ...'[2]

Some 30 parliamentary seats were in the control of the Treasury itself, and a large number of other seats were in the

---

[1] H. Roseveare, *The Treasury*, Allen Lane, 1969, p. 86.
[2] K. Lowenstein, *op. cit.*, p. 88.

gift of powerful aristocratic cliques or highly-placed individuals. Seats were bought and sold like livestock—most MPs being returned unopposed—and the votes of these 'representatives of the people' in the House were bought and sold through the patronage system.

With the House of Commons thus in its pocket, there was no independent parliamentary check on the government's expenditure and efficiency in the utilisation of resources. The House could not and did not function to restrain and prevent wasteful and extravagant government expenditure.

This situation provoked much furious public and academic criticism. Adam Smith's great work, *The Wealth of Nations* (1776), was but one influential commentary provoked by this situation. Smith charged that:

> 'It is the highest impertinence and presumption in kings and ministers to pretend to watch over the economy of private people and to restrain their expense either by sumptuary laws or by prohibiting the importation of foreign luxuries. They are themselves always and without any exception the greatest spendthrifts in society. Let them look well after their own expenses and they may safely trust private people with theirs. If their own extravagance does not ruin the state, that of their subjects never will.'

A second major comparison between the post-World War II and the pre-Classical situations concerns the matter of the burden of state-issued debt. The pre-Classical Mercantilists had theorised that the true burden of the National Debt occurs at the moment of its creation. In this climate of opinion it was not surprising that British governments during the 18th century should have seen little reason why they should impose taxation (which always incurred public displeasure) rather than issue debts to finance the sporadic military adventures upon which the British Crown engaged during that period. This notion, that the burden of the National Debt occurs solely at its time of creation, constituted the Keynesian 'New Orthodoxy' of public debt theory that emerged after 1943.[1]

Over the course of the 18th century, in this permissive intellectual climate of prevailing Mercantilist opinion, the British

---

[1] The primary statement of the Keynesian 'New Orthodoxy' position is contained in A. P. Lerner, 'Functional Finance and the Federal Debt', *Social Research*, February 1943. A critique of the Keynesian theory of public debt is in J. M. Buchanan, *Public Principles of Public Debt*, R. D. Irwin, Homewood, Ill., 1958; and J. M. Buchanan and R. E. Wagner, *Public Debt in Democratic Society*, American Enterprise Institute, Washington DC, 1967.

National Debt escalated over ten-fold before the outbreak of the Napoleonic wars. During those wars, from 1800-16, there was a further doubling of the size of state-issued debt. The cost of servicing the National Debt came to comprise almost half of the total volume of public expenditure. These trends and their consequences provoked loud public criticism. The British classical economists argued, in opposition to the Mercantilists, that public debt could constitute a burden on future generations (of taxpayers),[1] and cause other undesirable occurrences such as the emigration of productive factors (especially mobile non-human capital) to other, lower-tax environments. They also

> 'clearly perceived that borrowing allows government to increase its activities without voters being forced to consider the limits to government activity which they would prefer'.[2]

Consequently, the major British classical economists argued that governments should seek, and be caused, to balance their expenditure against their taxation. Most also argued that deficit finance was regretfully necessary in time of war, and appropriate in the singular case of long-lived public investments, such as roads and canals, which generate benefits for future generations. These classical arguments were to influence public and political thought profoundly.

The experiences of the 18th and early 19th centuries in Britain —of uncontrolled expenditure growth and escalating public debt—provoked a major backlash in public and academic opinion against the orthodox Mercantilist opinion of the preceding era. The new Classical ideas about the wastefulness of much government expenditure and the dangers of deficit finance found a ready audience. Serious politicians began to realise that major reform of the British fiscal constitution was necessary to check these clear failures of the public realm. Under the pressure of public and academic opinion, reform of the British fiscal constitution was eventually undertaken. Reforming Administrations of the 19th century sought to outlaw

---

[1] The only major dissenter from this view in the British Classical ranks was Lord Lauderdale: B. A. Corry, 'Lauderdale and the Public Debt—A Reconsideration', in M. Peston and B. A. Corry (eds.), *Essays in Honour of Lord Robbins,* Weidenfeld and Nicolson, 1972.

[2] D. P. O'Brien, *The Classical Economists,* Clarendon Press, 1975, Ch. 9, p. 262; also J. Burkhead, 'The Balanced Budget', *Quarterly Journal of Economics,* May 1954.

public corruption, to bring government expenditure under control, and to set up formal and effective accounting and control procedures for the public finances, culminating in Gladstone's administrative reforms of the 1860s.[1] Recourse to deficit finance for government expenditure, except under closely-defined circumstances, came to be viewed by public and government as an unwarranted, unacceptable, and shameful activity. The convention of a balanced budget, so necessary to offset the developing biases of the British constitution, came to be accepted as a fundamental principle of the British fiscal constitution.

The pressures towards excessive expenditure and deficit finance in the 19th century

Mid-20th-century popular mythology, informed by several decades of historically unrealistic Keynesian analysis of the British fiscal constitution, has leant towards the view that classical liberal economic thought embodied a simplistic, unbalanced, and rabid attack on government expenditure as such. Such a criticism rests on a misunderstanding. What the British classical economists sought to attack was the *wasteful* government expenditure and *unrestrained* recourse to deficit finance resulting from a fiscal constitution that provided an insufficient check against such phenomena. None of the classical economists attacked government expenditure *per se*, or government borrowing to finance it, under certain defined circumstances, specifically, wars and long-lived public investments. Why British classical economists argued for a balanced-budget rule (subject to these exceptions) was that they perceived a bias in the British fiscal constitution towards *excessive* government expenditure and deficit finance.

This bias clearly existed in the 18th century, and remained even under the balanced-budget rule—though checked—in the 19th century. The biases, and the fundamental role of the balanced-budget rule in providing a check upon them, are recorded by 19th-century commentators on the working of the British constitution.

In his classic work of 1867 on *The English Constitution*, Walter Bagehot noted that, since the time Parliament had won its struggles against the Crown for the control of the public

[1] F. W. Fetter and D. Gregory, *Government and Society in Nineteenth Century Britain: Monetary and Financial Policy*, Irish University Press, 1973.

purse, a change of fiscal attitude had taken place within the House:

'The House of Commons—now that it is the true sovereign, and appoints the executive—has long ceased to be the checking, sparing body it once was. It is now more apt to spend money than the Minister of the day ... The process is simple. Every expenditure of public money has some apparent public object; those who wish to spend the money expatiate on that object: they say, "What is £50,000 to this great country? Is this a time for cheeseparing objections? Our industry was never so productive; our resources never so immense. What is £50,000 in comparison with this great national interest?"
The members who are for the expenditure always come down; perhaps a constituent or a friend who will profit by the outlay, or is keen on the object, has asked them to attend; and, at any rate, there is always a popular vote to be given, on which the newspapers—always philanthropic, and sometimes talked over—will be sure to make encomiums.
The members against the expenditure rarely come down of themselves; why should they become unpopular without reason? The object seems decent; many of its advocates are certainly sincere; a hostile vote will make enemies, and be censured by the journals. *If there were not some check, the "people's house" would soon outrun the people's money.*'[1]

These constituency pressures for expenditure were backed, as they are today, by the forces of bureaucratic empire-building. A witness (Ralph Lingen) noted in his evidence to the Select Committee on Civil Service Expenditure in 1873 that 'each department under each minister is almost a little kingdom in itself': each departmental bureaucracy sought to maximise the size of its budget allocation, and strove to avoid any dimension of parliamentary interference in its affairs.[2]

Given these normal constituency and bureaucratic pressures, and the feeble ability of much of Britain's historically-evolved fiscal constitution to resist these pressures, what prevented 19th-century Britain from exhibiting the same fiscal behaviour as in the 18th century and in the recent post-World War II period? Another quotation from Bagehot illustrates the crucial role in

---

[1] W. Bagehot, *The English Constitution*, Fontana Library Edn., 1963, pp. 154-55 (italics added).

[2] An economic analysis of such bureaucratic behaviour is in W. A. Niskanen, *Bureaucracy: Servant or Master?*, Hobart Paperback 5, IEA, 1973.

SIGNIFICANCE—

The Importance of the Proposals for the British Reader

1 THE VOTER would have a clearer indication of the true cost of government spending. The 'fiscal illusion' of the voter, which governments seek to exploit, would be reduced. There would be an end to the politics of macro-economic 'auctioneering'.

2 THE HOUSE OF COMMONS would have to consider government expenditure and revenue jointly, not separately. The political consequences of increased government spending would have to be faced, because higher spending would mean higher taxation or increased charges. The House, not the Government, would have the power to waive the rule of budget balance, in times of national emergency.

3 THE TREASURY'S objectives would change. It would no longer try to manipulate the economy according to the dictates of its political masters. Its primary role—its historic role—would be re-established: the watchdog of the public purse. The Treasury's monitoring and control of government spending would be toughened.

4 THE CHANCELLOR OF THE EXCHEQUER would have the same ability as now to decide on the volume of government spending. But he would have to make the decision knowing that additional spending would require additional taxation or charges: which voters do not like. He would have a new incentive to choose carefully: the political disadvantages of higher taxation or charges would have to be balanced against the political benefits of increased government spending.

5 THE GOVERNMENT would no longer be able to manipulate the economy for its own political profit. The political stratagem of 'reflating' the economy before an election—of trying to buy votes by cutting taxes and increasing government spending—would no longer be possible.

6 THE BANK OF ENGLAND would be fully independent of the Government and the Treasury. But it would be subjected to a statutory requirement laid down by Parliament—that it must follow a fixed rule on the rate of growth of the money supply. The over-riding task of the Bank would be the control of the currency.

7 THE PUBLIC EXPENDITURE SURVEY COMMITTEE would no longer be able to indulge in the fanciful illusion that government expenditure can be decided without regard to government revenue. There would be the new realisation that government revenue is the *constraint* on government spending.

8 INDUSTRY AND COMMERCE would find that they were subjected to less economic instability caused by government. The economic environment of business planning would become more stable and predictable.

9 PRESSURE GROUPS that lobby the Government and the Chancellor for tax concessions and spending in their favour would find increased resistance to their suasion.

10 CIVIL SERVANTS would find much more cost-consciousness by their political masters, and more stringent controls on expenditure. There would be a new incentive to experiment with systems of charging as a means of raising revenue.

11 THE NATIONAL INSTITUTE OF ECONOMIC AND SOCIAL RESEARCH would have to find new economic games to play, or would have more difficulty justifying its Treasury and Social Science Research Council grants. J.B.

the 19th-century British fiscal constitution of the balanced-budget convention:

> 'That check [on the 'people's house' outrunning the people's money] is the responsibility of the Cabinet for the national finance. If anyone could propose a tax, they might let the House spend as it would... but now... the Ministry must find the money. Accordingly, they have *the strongest motive to oppose extra outlay*. They will have to pay the bill for it; *they will have to impose taxation*, which is always disagreeable, or suggest loans, which, under ordinary circumstances, are shameful.'[1]

This passage thus also demonstrates clearly the fundamental change that has taken place in the British fiscal constitution since Bagehot's day, as a result of the Keynesian revolution in economic policy. Why should the Cabinet any longer 'oppose extra outlay'? Is government borrowing now regarded as a 'shameful' activity? What strange word is that? To say the very least, such expressions do not accord well with the reality of British governmental behaviour in the post-war period.

This difference in behaviour between Bagehot's day and ours is simple to explain. The British *government* acted as a check on the expenditure and deficit biases of the political system because, in Bagehot's day, it had to pay the political bills. Under the balanced-budget convention, with deficit finance ruled out, extra expenditure meant extra taxation. There was a powerful electoral incentive to efficient and economic expenditure by the Cabinet and government. Today, under the Keynesian fiscal constitution, that convention no longer exists. Government can now increase its expenditure without raising —indeed, often simultaneously *reducing*—its tax revenue, simply by bridging the deficiency in the public finances by issuing money or creating new debt.

Keynes and his disciples argued in the 20th century that the balanced-budget principle was some unthinking Victorian moral code that had nothing whatsoever to do with the rational conduct of government affairs. In his pamphlet *Can Lloyd George Do It?*, Keynes implied that adherence to this fiscal principle was the dotardly habit of mind of 'nothing but a few old gentlemen in tightly buttoned-up frock coats, who only need to be treated with a little friendly disrespect and bowled over

---

[1] Bagehot, *op. cit.*, p. 155 (italics added).

like ninepins'.[1] He could not have been more wildly wrong in this assumption. The balanced-budget principle played a crucial role in holding the pre-Keynesian fiscal constitution together, and constraining the otherwise inherent biases of that system to over-expenditure and deficit finance. Once the balanced-budget had been bowled over by the Keynesian revolution, those biases were unleashed. There was nothing else in the fiscal constitution to stop them.

c. THE PRESUPPOSITIONS OF JOHN MAYNARD KEYNES

John Maynard Keynes was born in 1883, the son of a Cambridge don and the city's first woman councillor (later its mayor). The family home in Harvey Road, Cambridge, provided an environment of academic values and Victorian upper-middle class notions of public duty. What were the 'presuppositions of Harvey Road' to be embedded in Keynes's own later policy prescriptions?

(1) *'The public interest'*: This is the assumption that policy decisions are undertaken by intelligent people acting on the basis of a rational evaluation of the public interest. Thus, for instance, in the 'twenties,

> 'When Keynes advocated [in place of the Gold Standard] a "managed" currency, the Treasury asked him pertinently how he would prevent inflation. His answer in effect was: by the exercise of responsible intelligence. Sir Roy Harrod rightly remarks that "Keynes . . . deemed England a sufficiently mature country for it to be possible to assume that the authorities . . . would not indulge in an orgy of feckless note issues".'[2]

An alternative hypothesis of political and bureaucratic behaviour is offered in this *Paper*.[3] It is also interesting to note that this Keynesian presupposition stands curiously in relation to many of Keynes's personal observations of the behaviour and antics of politicians, which he was well placed to watch as an important civil servant during both the First and Second World Wars. In 1911, in a letter to the artist, Duncan Grant,

[1] J. M. Keynes and H. Henderson, 'Can Lloyd George Do It?', *The Collected Writings of John Maynard Keynes*, Vol. IX, St. Martins Press, 1972, p. 125.

[2] R. Skidelsky, 'The Political Meaning of the Keynesian Revolution', *Spectator*, 7 August, 1976, p. 9.

[3] Gordon Tullock, *The Vote Motive*, Hobart Paperback 9, IEA, 1976, discusses the elements of the economics of politics.

Keynes says 'you haven't, I suppose, ever mixed with politicians at close quarters . . . they're awful . . . their stupidity is inhuman'.[1] At many other points in his voluminous writings, he records his disdainful view of politicians, calling them 'madmen in authority', 'near to earth', 'lunatics', and the like.

How, then, did Keynes reconcile his personal impression of *homo politicus* with a presumption that they would always be able to identify the public interest and act single-mindedly upon it? At some points in his own writing, Keynes gives an impression that he realised there was a flaw or inconsistency in his assumptions about political behaviour and human behaviour generally. Two years after the *General Theory* was published he wrote that ' . . . I still suffer incurably from attributing an unreal rationality to other people's feelings and behaviour (and doubtless my own too)'.[2] Perhaps part of the solution to this apparent inconsistency also lies in the other two presuppositions.

(2) *The philosopher-king hypothesis of the British ruling élite:* Keynes implicitly assumed that the control of the British political system ultimately lay in the hands of an intellectual élite of civil servants and others drawn from the same upper-middle-class and public school/Oxbridge-educated background, all deeply imbued with the same notions of the public duty as himself. Thus, 'the government of Britain would be in the hands of an intellectual aristocracy using the methods of persuasion'.[3] This presumption, that the governance of Britain could be safely entrusted to an élite of bureaucrats of a 'liberal, moral' outlook, is neatly captured in a letter Keynes wrote to Professor F. A. Hayek in 1944 (concerning *The Road to Serfdom*):

'I should say that what we want is not no planning, or even less planning, indeed I should say that we almost certainly want more. But the planning should take place in a community in which as many people as possible, both leaders and followers, wholly share your own liberal moral position. Moderate planning will be safe if those carrying it out are rightly orientated in their own minds and hearts to the moral issue . . . dangerous acts can be done safely in a community which thinks and feels rightly, which

[1] Quoted in R. Skidelsky, 'Keynes and the Revolt against the Victorians', *Spectator*, 1 May, 1976, p. 15.

[2] John Maynard Keynes, 'My Early Beliefs', *The Collected Writings of John Maynard Keynes*, Vol. X, St. Martins Press, p. 488.

[3] D. E. Moggridge, *Keynes*, Fontana, 1976, p. 38.

would be the way to hell if they were executed by those who think and feel wrongly.'[1]

As this passage so eloquently demonstrates, Keynes never faced up to Professor Karl Popper's 'Problem': what if the élite turn out *not* to be benevolent Philosopher-Kings? Nor did he seriously consider the structure of constitutional checks and balances, and political rewards and costs, that are necessary to prevent the misuse or abuse of political and bureaucratic power. As the power was assumed to be wielded by an intellectually-inclined benevolent élite, he did not need to consider such problems.

(3) *The élite's power of persuasion:* Keynes believed that the élite could, and should, manipulate public opinion in the manner desired so as to conform to its policy prescriptions.[2] As Professor Hayek argues, Keynes was perhaps rather too influenced here by his own self-confidence:

'. . . he was really supremely confident of his powers of persuasion and believed that he could play on public opinion as a virtuoso plays on his instrument'.[3]

Professor Hayek also reports that the last time he saw Keynes, in 1946,

'I had asked him whether he was not getting alarmed about the use to which some of his disciples were putting his theories. His reply was that these theories had been greatly needed in the 1930s, but if these theories should ever become harmful, I could be assured that he would quickly bring about a change in public opinion'.[4]

It seems that Keynes forgot his own most famous phrase—'in the long run we are all dead'. A few weeks after this revealing discussion, Keynes suffered a fatal heart attack. A surfeit of self-confidence is perhaps understandable in a brilliant man. A presumption of immortality is not.

The Bloomsbury View

In 1903, Keynes joined the Apostles, a small and secretive Cambridge society, from whose ranks many of the members of

[1] Quoted in D. E. Moggridge, *ibid.*, p. 44.

[2] Moggridge, pp. 38-40.

[3] F. A. Hayek, *A Tiger by the Tail: The Keynesian Legacy of Inflation*, Hobart Paperback 4, IEA, 1972 (2nd Edn., 1978), pp. 103-4.

[4] F. A. Hayek, *ibid.*, p. 103.

[49]

the famous Bloomsbury Group were also later drawn. The ideas that Keynes drew from both associations significantly supplemented his presuppositions of Harvey Road. Keynes summarised the thought of these groups in the following fashion:

'We entirely repudiated a personal liability on us to obey general rules. We claimed the right to judge every individual case on its merits, and the wisdom, experience, and self-control to do so successfully. This was a very important part of our faith, violently and aggressively held . . . we repudiated entirely customary morals, conventions, and traditional wisdom. . . We . . . believe in a continuing moral progress by virtue of which the human race already consists of reliable, rational, decent folk, influenced by truth and objective standards, who can safely be released from the outward restraints of convention and traditional standards and inflexible rules of conduct, and left, from now onwards, to their own sensible devices, pure motives and reliable intuitions of the good.'[1]

This Bloomsbury View would seem to underlie or permeate much of Keynes's general attitudes to economic and public policy generally. He seemed to view the balanced-budget idea as a mere inflexible rule of governmental conduct, a Victorian convention without functional political significance. And, given that people—or at least the élite that he supposed to control and manipulate them—have 'pure motives and reliable intuitions of the good', the breaching of such a constitutional convention gave him no cause for concern.

The dentist model of the economic adviser

From his presuppositions of Harvey Road and his Bloomsbury View of the world, Keynes derived his notions of the potentialities of economics in the formation of policy, and the role of economic advisers in that process. In 1929 he called for the creation of an 'Economic General Staff'—a body of economic experts that would

'mark . . . a first measure towards the deliberate and purposive guidance of the evolution of our economic life . . . a recognition of the enormous part to be played in this by the scientific spirit as distinct from purely party political attitude, which is never more out of place than in relation to complex matters of fact and interpretation regarding technical difficulty . . .'[2]

---

[1] Keynes, 'My Early Beliefs', *op. cit.*, pp. 435-7.

[2] Quoted in E. S. Johnson and H. G. Johnson, 'The Social and Intellectual Origins of the General Theory', *History of Political Economy*, Vol. 6, 1974, p. 265.

Thus, Keynes foresaw economists in government acting in a manner analogous to 'dentists'—technicians who would operate skilfully to repair economic malfunctioning. The economic adviser would offer unbiased, scientific advice, which decision-makers would then act on in the public interest. Keynes foresaw knowledge of the workings of the economy, presented by dentist-economists to decision-makers acting on 'pure' motives, as bringing about an era of 'joy through statistics'.[1]

D. THE KEYNESIAN BRITISH FISCAL CONSTITUTION—IN THEORY

In numerous newspaper articles, speeches and pamphlets in the 'twenties and early 'thirties, Keynes called for deficit-financed public works expenditures as a cure for unemployment. He brushed off as a 'bogy' the possibility that this could, or would, lead to inflation: 'There is no reason why we should not feel ourselves free to be bold, to be open, to experiment, to take action, to try the possibilities of things.'[2]

The *General Theory* (1936) attempted to provide a theoretical foundation for such views. But it did not make plain the precise implication of this analysis for economic policy.[3] It contains the odd scornful aside on Gladstonian finance as 'penny-wisdom' (p. 362), a cryptic call for 'a somewhat comprehensive socialisation of investment' (p. 378), a neo-Mercantilist proposition that real wealth increases/decreases as the supply of gold increases/decreases (the effects of which can then be simulated by public works financed by fiat money creation) (pp. 129-30), and a general indication that aggregate output and employment could, and should, be determined by fiscal and interest-rate policies (p. 378). One of Keynes's followers, Hugh Dalton, argued that in

> '*The Means to Prosperity* [published 1933] Keynes was still for balancing the budget over a period longer than one year. But in

---

[1] Quoted in D. E. Moggridge, *op. cit.*, p. 126.

[2] John Maynard Keynes and H. Henderson, 'Can Lloyd George Do It?', *op. cit.*, pp. 118-25.

[3] The Oxford economist Hubert Henderson—who had written the 'Can Lloyd George Do It?' pamphlet with Keynes in 1929—sternly criticised the *General Theory* as being 'incoherent' in its policy implications: H. D. Henderson, 'Mr. Keynes's Theories', in H. Clay (ed.), *The Inter-War Years and Other Papers: A Selection from the Writings of Hubert Douglas Henderson*, Clarendon Press, 1955, p. 167.

the *General Theory* he has freed himself and his policies of any such limitation'.[1]

None of this, however, constituted a very adequate or detailed specification of a Keynesian monetary-fiscal constitution.

This latter task was taken up not by Keynes himself but, rather, by his disciples—members of the 'Cambridge Circus' (such as Meade) who had worked over the drafts of the *General Theory* with him, and other converts to Keynesian analysis, in the following years. The writings of these disciples show how the Keynesian monetary-fiscal constitution was supposed to work in Keynesian theory.

(i) *Meade*

In his *Economic Analysis and Policy*, published soon after the *General Theory*, James Meade (Nobel Economics Prize Winner, 1977) provided a detailed specification of a Keynesian policy régime.[2] The government, he proposed, should act to stabilise the level of output and employment by a policy of budget balance over the trade cycle—'a government should budget for a large surplus in good times and for a small surplus or a deficit in bad times' (p. 44)—reinforced by contra-cyclical variations in monetary policy and interest rates, and in the volume of consumer 'credits' issued as part of an unemployment compensation scheme. These

> 'foregoing proposals must be sharply distinguished from an attempt to finance an ordinary budget deficit by inflationary measures. For if a government finances a permanent budget deficit by printing more paper money this must lead to a progressive and inflationary rise in prices'. (p. 54)

Professor Meade also argued that there was a 'standard' rate of unemployment in the economy, which was determined by the real forces of the economic system, such as the size of search and information costs and other factors. No attempt should be made by government to reduce unemployment below this 'standard' level by fiscal/monetary policy. The 'standard' rate could only be reduced if policies designed to 'improve the organisation of the labour market' were employed (p. 77). Trade union action would raise the standard rate, if they pushed

---

[1] H. Dalton, *Principles of Public Finance*, Routledge and Kegan Paul, 1954, p. 221, fn. 1.

[2] J. E. Meade, *Economic Analysis and Policy*, Oxford University Press, 2nd Edn., 1938.

wages up in spite of heavy unemployment, as would payment of unemployment benefit on generous scales. The government should estimate this standard rate, and set contractionary monetary and fiscal policies in motion when unemployment fell below that level.

Thus Meade, the Keynesian, was arguing in the late 'thirties in very similar vein to Milton Friedman, the monetarist, in his famous 'natural rate of unemployment' hypothesis expressed some three decades later.[1]

(ii) *Dalton*

In his *Principles of Public Finance*, Hugh Dalton sought to detail the implications of the Keynesian revolution for the theory and practice of public finance.[2] Although not a member of the Cambridge Circus, Dalton was strongly influenced by Keynesian thought, and was Britain's first Chancellor of the Exchequer in the post-war Keynesian era (1945-47).

Dalton proposed that:

> 'we may now free ourselves from the old and narrow conception of balancing the budget, no matter over what period, and move towards the new and wider conception of budget balancing over the whole economy.' (p.221)

This seemingly open-ended recipe was, however, carefully qualified by Dalton. In the long run, the budget 'clearly' must be balanced, 'unless we are prepared to contemplate an increase, unlimited in time and amount, of the deadweight debt' (p. 216). Such a prospect was 'clearly intolerable', 'indefensible' and 'an economic evil'. Even in the short run (to be measured in terms of a year or two), the imbalance of the budget 'must not be excessive', for if 'deficits are so large as to give the sense of a financial situation out of control, the results may be very damaging' (p.217).

[1] Cf. M. Friedman, 'The Role of Monetary Policy', *American Economic Review*, Vol. 58, 1968. There are differences between the Meade standard rate hypothesis and the Friedman natural rate hypothesis. In particular—and this is a crucial difference—Meade, as with other Keynesians of that time, implicitly assumed that employees are concerned with the money value of their wages, and that money wages would show no tendency to rise if unemployment were higher than the standard rate. Friedman argues that employees are concerned for their *real* incomes, and thus will be influenced by expectations about future price-levels in their money wage bargaining.

[2] H. Dalton, *Principles of Public Finance*, Routledge & Kegan Paul, 1st Edn., 1922, 4th Edn., 1954. All page references here cited are to the latter edition.

Elements of the American Keynesian New Orthodoxy of public debt theory appeared in Dalton's *Principles*, but this was counter-balanced by arguments that public debt should not be created lightly. He saw debt finance of a budget deficit as likely to involve transfers of an inegalitarian character, to reward inherited wealth at the expense of work and productive risk-taking, resulting in losses of potential production. Dalton's treatment of deficit finance *via* money creation is almost pure Hayek. The attempt to raise government revenue *via* the printing press would only generate a 'temporary and unhealthy stimulus' to the economy, leading to 'miscalculations and misdirection of resources', with a long-run prospect of economic and political upheaval if continued indefinitely.

However, Dalton implicitly assumed that politicians would adhere to his prescriptions, so that fears of chronic budget deficits under a Keynesian fiscal constitution were 'irrational'. He regarded politicians as trustees of future generations, who should 'aim at making a more general provision for the future than would be made by private individuals left to themselves' (p. 16). Dalton seemed to be unaware that his normative views of what politicians *should* do might not correspond with reality. In particular, he ignored the strong political incentives for democratic governments to discount the future very heavily, once the balanced-budget rule is destroyed.

(iii) *Kaldor*

In his appendix to Sir William Beveridge's famous *Full Employment in a Free Society*, Professor Lord Kaldor set out the implications of the adoption of a full-employment policy for Britain.[1]

Professor Kaldor argued that a Keynesian full-employment policy was quite consistent with a régime of budget surpluses rather than budget deficits, so long as a situation of secular stagnation did not emerge after World War II. Indeed, he thought that an inflationary gap problem (necessitating recourse to a budget surplus) might typify the immediate post-war period. *If* a situation of secular stagnation emerged thereafter, we might then 'have to reckon with a steadily rising

[1] N. Kaldor, Appendix C of *Full Employment in a Free Society*, by Sir William Beveridge, Allen & Unwin, 1944, reprinted as 'The Quantitative Aspects of the Full Employment Problem in Britain', in N. Kaldor, *Essays on Economic Policy*, Vol. I, Duckworth, 1964. All page references he recited are to the latter source.

public debt in peacetime'. Lord Kaldor's vision of this possible scenario was tinged with elements of the Keynesian new orthodoxy, but at the same time he warned that increasing public debt might reduce the incentive for some to work and to save (as a result of an increasing *rentier* element in their income streams). In any case, he viewed the prospect of an increasing National Debt generating a steadily increasing burden as highly unlikely. It could only be the case

'with a rate of borrowing far in excess of anything that might be necessary under peacetime conditions in order to sustain a full employment policy'. (p. 81)

Professor Kaldor also assumed that 'post-war governments will pursue a monetary and wage policy which maintains the prices of final commodities constant', as 'a policy of a rising price level might be incompatible with the maintenance of stability in the long run' (p. 79).

Conclusion

The analyses of Meade, Dalton and Kaldor illustrate how Keynes and his disciples presumed that a Keynesian monetary-fiscal constitution would work. They presumed a régime of 'functional finance' with budget balance over the cycle (unless a situation of secular stagnation was encountered). Budget surplus would follow and offset budget deficit as the trade cycle oscillated. Even in the short run, recourse to deficit finance would be careful and moderate, not excessive and damaging. There would be a policy of long-run monetary and price-level stability. Governments would not attempt to reduce unemployment below its estimated equilibrium rate. Political decision-makers, acting under the guidance of professional economists, and acting as the trustees of future generations, would fully take into account the long-run consequences of their current fiscal-monetary actions, at a socially-optimal rate of time discount. Public debt would not be lightly created.[1]

[1] There are some indications that Keynes himself was, towards the end of his life, becoming less enamoured with the idealised visions of a régime of functional finance, as painted by his followers. One such indication is the revealing discussion between Hayek and Keynes (quoted above, p. 49). Another is to be found in a letter written by Keynes to Professor F. Machlup in 1944: 'Functional Finance is an idea and not a policy; part of one's apparatus of thought but not, except highly diluted under a considerable clothing of qualification, an apparatus of action. Economists have to try to be very careful, I think, to distinguish the two.' (Quoted in D. E. Moggridge, 'Keynes: The Economist', in D. E. Moggridge (ed.), *Keynes, Aspects of the Man and his Work*, Macmillan, 1974, p. 59.)

How does this anticipated scenario of the workings of the Keynesian British monetary-fiscal constitution compare with the reality of the post-war period?

E. THE KEYNESIAN BRITISH FISCAL CONSTITUTION— IN REALITY

The contrast between the Keynesian *presumptions* described above and the *reality* of British monetary and fiscal experience in the post-war period is nothing short of startling.

There has been no policy of long-run stability in money supply and prices. There has been precious little attempt by the Bank of England to control the volume of 'high-powered' money (*i.e.*, that component of the money stock issued by the central bank, which determines the total amount of the money supply).[1] Inflation has been persistent in Britain throughout the post-war period, and chronic in recent years. There has been no governmental attempt in the post-war period to estimate the equilibrium rate of unemployment, and to pursue Keynesian contractionary policies when unemployment fell below it. There has been an almost continuous attempt to reduce unemployment by monetary, fiscal and other means to the lowest achievable number, so that, for most of the period, registered unemployment seldom rose above 1-$1\frac{1}{2}$ per cent of the total labour force.[2] There has been no contra-cyclical variation of the level of government expenditure; rather, it has grown almost continuously. There has been no offsetting variation over time of budget deficits and surpluses, but rather persistent deficits (except as in 1969-70, when the Treasury was acting under the watchful eye of the IMF). Yet there has been no secular stagnation to justify such a policy of persistent deficit finance. Until 1973-74, the post-war period saw economic expansion in Britain and the world economy generally.

Clearly, on any reckoning of the evidence, the contemporary Keynesian monetary-fiscal constitution of Great Britain has not worked out in practice in the way that Keynes and his

---

[1] Shadow European Economic Policy Committee, 'Statement by the Paris Watchdogs', *Banker*, July 1977, p. 35.

[2] The defects of registered unemployment totals as economic and social indicators have been analysed by J. B. Wood, *How Much Unemployment?*, Research Monograph 28, IEA, 1972, and *How Little Unemployment?*, Hobart Paper 65, IEA, 1975.

followers anticipated. Many Keynesians now admit this failure. As Professor Joan Robinson has said:

'... it has all turned out to be a daydream. The twenty-five years after the war that passed without a major recession has been called the Age of Keynes, but it was not much like his vision. It turned out close to Kalecki's sardonic description of the régime of the political trade cycle.'[1]

The fundamental flaw of the Keynesian daydream was its implicit unrealistic assumptions about political and bureaucratic behaviour, flowing ultimately from the presuppositions of Harvey Road and the Bloomsbury View. This flaw was buttressed by an academic failure of the Keynesians to reflect on the historical and intellectual origins of the 19th-century balanced-budget rule, and to appreciate its constitutional significance and necessity. Given the development of parliamentary parties in the 18th and 19th centuries, the other elements of the British 19th-century fiscal constitutional (rules 1 to 6, pp. 37-38) provided no safeguard against the manipulation of the budget by a parliamentary majority for political profit. The balanced-budget convention was necessary to check that inherent bias. The effect of the Keynesian revolution was to remove that lynchpin of the British fiscal constitution. The other conventions of the British 19th-century fiscal constitution remain to this day. But with its mooring-rope cut, there was nothing to stop the drift towards the growth of expenditure and the running-up of budget deficits in the British political system. That drift is clearly demonstrated in Table II.

Keynesian presuppositions v. Whitehall/Westminster realpolitik

The Keynesian presuppositions—of public-interest maximising politicians and officials, acting as far-sighted statesmen and trustees of the future—simply do not square with the realities of contemporary (or earlier) British political and bureaucratic life.

First, political decision-makers do not adopt some grand Daltonian 'trustees of the future' time perspective. The reality is much closer to what might be called a 'Wilsonian' time-perspective in policy-making.[2] Sir Alec Cairncross, who had

---

[1] Joan Robinson, 'What Has Become of the Keynesian Revolution?', in J. Robinson (ed.), *After Keynes*, Basil Blackwell, 1973, p. 10.

[2] After ex-Premier (now Sir) Harold Wilson's perhaps most famous adage: 'A week in politics is a long time'.

much experience of this telescoped perspective from close observation as Head of the Government Economic Service from 1964 to 1969, describes the reality:

'In democratic society governments have an uncertain length of life and hesitate to curtail it deliberately by giving precedence to long-run gains at the cost of short-run unpopularity. They are to some extent in the same situation as companies exposed to the threat of take-over in that there is a premium on action conferring clear and immediate benefits.

Economic myopia of this kind does not, however, deter governments from taking large risks with considerable light-heartedness. For they may enter into commitments involving heavy eventual outlays so long as they either win immediate credit or escape from awkward political dilemmas or gratify some critical section of opinion.'[1]

Second, public decisions are not made by Philosopher-Kings maximising the public interest on the basis of a theory of optimal economic policy, Keynesian or otherwise. They are made by politicians concerned (like the rest of us) with the security of their jobs. They have a strong motive to avoid actions that lose support amongst Cabinet colleagues, party ranks, or voters generally, even if these actions generate long-run benefits to society. To quote Sir Alec Cairncross again:

'It is . . . naive to think that a Chancellor should frame his Budget without first asking whether it would commend itself to the Cabinet, to the Party, or to the House of Commons as currently constituted . . .

. . . decisions of policy are influenced more by consideration of prestige, loss of face, announcement effects, immediate negotiability, and so on, and less by ultimate economic advantage . . .

. . . there is no such thing as economic policy in isolation from other aspects of policy . . . there is only policy.'[2]

Third, the role of the economic adviser in the politico-bureaucratic machine is not that of an impartial technician imparting professional knowledge that guides and steers political choices amongst policy options so as to maximise social welfare. Such a world, as Professor A. T. Peacock has urbanely noted, 'does not exist':

[1] Alec Cairncross, 'The Managed Economy', in A. Cairncross (ed.), *The Managed Economy*, Basil Blackwell, 1970, p. 15.

[2] *Ibid.*, pp. 20-22.

'The role of the economist as the impartial, cautious technical observer always appealing to the evidence cuts little ice with politicians and administrators thirsting for action . . . policies will be instituted despite the warnings of the economist about the strong assumptions on which they are based . . .'[1]

An economist confronting a policy-maker with 'politically unacceptable' evidence or analysis, as Professor Peacock also records, is likely to be made 'uncomfortably aware' of the inexactness of his discipline, and to suffer comparisons with more 'acceptable' advice from other sources. Indeed:

'A minister may be so committed to his own view of what policies are "right" that he will instruct his officials to prepare for him a persuasive case, whatever doubts there may be about the support these policies receive from economic analysis and the related empirical evidence.'[2]

Confronted with this *reality* of the politico-bureaucratic process, the economic adviser can either, as Professor Peacock notes, 'pack his bags and try to practise his skills elsewhere', or eventually, as Dr Turvey records, 'one does not waste everyone's time by putting up suggestions which are not going to be acceptable'.[3]

These judgements were all made by eminent economists with experience in the highest echelons of the decision-making process of British government and public administration. The off-the-record, private observations of economists with experience of government tend to be even harsher, ranging from 'masters of deception' to 'outright frauds'. So much, therefore, for the 'dentist model' of the economic adviser.

The observations of contemporary politicians themselves also clearly reveal the pressures and incentives that exist in government, parliament, and the civil service towards the expansion of public expenditure and deficit finance. Two American academics, Professors Heclo and Wildavsky, summarising the results of many exclusive and anonymous interviews with politicians and administrators, record:

[1] Alan Peacock, 'Giving Economic Advice in Difficult Times', *Three Banks Review*, March 1977, p. 8.

[2] *Ibid.*, p. 13.

[3] R. Turvey, 'The Economist in the Public Service', in K. J. W. Alexander, A. G. Kemp, and T. M. Rybzynski (eds.), *The Economist in Business*, Basil Blackwell, 1967, p. 159.

'Inside his department, the spending minister who is uninterested in increased spending is likely to be viewed, if not with distaste, at least with despair . . . Ministerial responsibility means that the department's successes and failures are also his own. The normal way to gain respect and advance himself is to enhance some of the great purposes of his department. And great purposes usually cost money.'[1]

The incentive for a spending minister is, therefore, to expand his programmes, and to avoid cuts—without regard for any theories of economic policy or for total budget size. A former Socialist (Labour) Secretary of State in a big spending department (education) has described the outcome of these incentives or pressures as

'an endless tactical battle [for more resources] which requires determination, cunning and occasional unscrupulousness. In an ideal world it would all no doubt be settled by some omniscient central unit, but this is the way it happens in our crude democratic world.'[2]

These bureaucratic and ministerial pressures towards increased expenditure are further reinforced by constituency level pressures. A Liberal MP tells us:

'Never a day goes by without my constituents writing at least half-a-dozen letters devising new ways of spending more public money. My constituents constantly ask me to spend money, and to be honest, I do not always think of it as mine, and so it goes on being spent.'[3]

Such lobbying pressures for higher expenditure and lower taxes also continuously assail the Chancellor of the Exchequer. As a former Conservative Chancellor describes it:

'. . . during the months of December, January and February the Chancellor receives a plethora of representations from Members of Parliament and from organisations with special interests and a wealth of good advice from all and sundry. The Financial Secretary is kept busy receiving delegations. All have one factor in common—an insistent demand for a reduction in one or more

---

[1] H. Heclo and A. Wildavsky, *The Private Government of Public Money*, Macmillan, 1974, p. 135.

[2] The late Anthony Crosland, then speaking as Secretary of State for Education, quoted in M. Kogan (ed.), *The Politics of Education*, Penguin, 1971, p. 167.

[3] John Pardoe, 'Political Pressures and Democratic Institutions', in *The Dilemmas of Government Expenditure*, IEA Readings No. 15, IEA, 1976, p. 79.

taxes or duties, or for an increase in one or more items of public expenditure—often both at the same time'.[1]

These are the realities of British democracy as seen from Whitehall and Westminster. To say the least, they are realities that do not correspond to Keynes's presuppositions of Harvey Road and 'the Bloomsbury View'.

f. The Failure of Remedial Measures

That there has been, throughout the post-war period, a persistent and seemingly uncontrollable tendency for government expenditure to rise has not gone without public notice, some governmental concern, or even without attempts at remedial action. These attempts have mainly been two: the Plowden measures of 1961, and the crisis measures of 1976. How did the first attempt fare, and what is likely to become of the second?

Plowden and PESC, 1961: an attempt at reform

By the late 1950s it had become clear that Britain's Keynesian fiscal constitution was not working as expected, in at least two main ways. First, the original statements of the Keynesian theory of economic policy in the 1930s by Keynes and his British followers had put most emphasis on variations on the *expenditure* side of the budget as a stabilisation device, and much less upon counter-cyclical variations on the *tax* side. It came to be increasingly realised, however, that much of government expenditure is of a long-term character, requiring lengthy pre-planning, and is not amenable to short-term macro-economic management.[2] Second, there was increasing concern at the way in which government expenditure always seemed to drift inexorably upwards. The Plowden Committee, set up to consider the general question of government expenditure, noted that 'the central problem is that of how to bring the growth of public expenditure under better control'.[3]

The Plowden Report (1961) detected no fundamental defect in the British fiscal system. All that was needed was a little more 'co-ordination' and 'planning'—the usual British civil service

---

[1] The Rt. Hon. Viscount Amory, 'Preparing the Budget', *Parliamentary Affairs*, Vol. XIV, 1960-61, pp. 455-6.

[2] J. C. R. Dow, *The Management of the British Economy 1945-60*, Cambridge University Press, 1964, Chs. VII and VIII.

[3] *The Control of Public Expenditure*, Cmnd. 1432, HMSO, July 1961, para. 6.

solutions for any and every problem. Plowden's solutions for
the two problems noted above were that Keynesian short-term
macro-management techniques needed to be supplemented by
departmentally-co-ordinated and medium-term forecasting and
planning of government expenditure.

> 'The basic idea was . . . that important decisions involving future
> public expenditure should be taken in the light of regular surveys
> of public expenditure as a whole, over a period of years, and in
> relation to prospective resources.'[1]

It is significant here to note that by 'prospective resources'
Plowden meant national output and not governmental revenue
from taxation, nor from user charges, which the Report did not
consider.[2]

Subsequently, the British system for the planning and control
of public expenditure was reformed in line with the conclusions
of the Plowden Report. This is known as the 'PESC' system,
(the inter-departmental Public Expenditure Survey Committee
that co-ordinates the forward-planning exercise). The first
medium-term expenditure survey was undertaken in 1961, and
later appeared intermittently until 1969, whereafter it was
published annually. The PESC system was greeted with wide-
spread acclaim. In the early 'seventies, a major Treasury
official recorded the view that 'this complex and sophisticated
system . . . ' has 'like all good instruments . . . shown its versa-
tility in use',[3] and that it was *comprehensive, consistent, sophisticated, dynamic, operational* and *strategic*'.[4] Professors Heclo and
Wildavsky also claimed that 'no nation in the world can match
the sophistication or thoroughness found in the British [PESC]
process of expenditure projection'.[5]

The PESC system is certainly elaborate. But it completely
failed to remedy the fundamental flaw of Britain's Keynesian
fiscal constitution—the inherent bias towards expenditure

---

[1] Sir Richard Clarke, 'Parliament and Public Expenditure', *Political Quarterly*,
Vol. 44, 1973, p. 137.

[2] Ralph Harris and Arthur Seldon, *Pricing or Taxing?*, Hobart Paper 71, IEA,
1976.

[3] Sir Samuel Goldman, *The Developing System of Public Expenditure Management and
Control*, Civil Service College Occasional Paper No. 2, HMSO, 1973.

[4] Sir Samuel Goldman, 'New Techniques in Government Budgeting: The
Presentation of Public Expenditure Proposals to Parliament', *Public Administration*, Autumn 1970, p. 254 (italics in original).

[5] H. Heclo and A. Wildavsky, *op. cit.*, p. 202.

growth and deficit finance. Indeed, it exacerbated that bias in a number of ways—as could have been predicted in 1961, on the basis of an elementary application of micro-economic analysis to political behaviour.[1]

The PESC system revolves around a forecast of total government expenditure in real terms over the following five years, given governmental policy commitments over that horizon. The assumption is that this procedure allows a decision on the appropriate size of government expenditure in relation to forecast national output over the medium term in the light of macro-management objectives, and the co-ordination of departmental spending programmes in line with that broad decision.

The PESC system certainly *allows* of such a decision. What is at fault is that it also contains hidden, latter-day versions of the presuppositions of Harvey Road, the Bloomsbury View, and the dentist model of the economic adviser. It assumes that governmental economic advisers are reasonably omniscient beings whose forecasts are not subject to political and bureaucratic pressures, and that politicians and administrators are long-sighted, public-interest maximising individuals who act as trustees of the future. If these implicit assumptions of the PESC system are replaced with contrary assumptions, it is likely to exacerbate the inherent bias of a Keynesian fiscal constitution.

The PESC system requires two forecasts: of the prospective movement of GDP, and of total government expenditure, both in real terms over a five-year horizon. The latter is based on a specification of existing governmental policy commitments involving government expenditure, and their projected resource costs during the forecasting horizon as estimated at the base-date. The defects of such a method of 'controlling' government expenditure are mainly six.

First, and most fundamentally, it puts the emphasis entirely on the expenditure side of the budget. There is no implication or assumption in PESC that extra spending requires extra taxation; it is simply assumed that the planned growth of expenditure will be financed 'somehow' (perhaps by extra public borrowing). The PESC system, therefore, embodies a

---

[1] The only major public figure to have comprehended the defects of PESC on this basis in 1961 was apparently Mr Enoch Powell; see his private letter to the then Chancellor, reprinted in D. Galloway, *The Public Prodigals*, Temple Smith, 1976, pp. 154-55.

fundamental bias towards expenditure growth, because governments are not forced to consider the electoral costs arising from higher taxation. As one of the anonymous authors of the Plowden Report later realised, 'in order to get realistic expenditure decisions, governments must argue them, both within themselves and outside, against their tax implications'.[1] Because it failed to correct this fundamental defect of Britain's post-war Keynesian fiscal constitution, the PESC reform was from its very inception doomed to fail in the Plowden goal of bringing government expenditure under control.

Second, the PESC system generates a political incentive for over-estimation of the projected growth of GDP. As future government expenditure is planned in relation to 'prospective resources', there is a temptation for politicians and forecasters to indulge in optimistic projections of the growth rate of the economy.[2] The planned growth in government expenditure can be made to look less prodigal simply by raising the forecast growth rate of output on paper. It is, therefore, no surprise to discover that PESC has provoked over-optimism about the performance of the economy, as during 1964-68 and 1974-75.[3] Furthermore, as government expenditure is planned and committed years ahead on the basis of optimistic growth forecasts, there is a persistent tendency for the volume of government expenditure to bulk larger in relation to total output, when the 'paper' growth-rates fail to materialise.

Third, there is a similar incentive to under-forecast the future *costs* of policy commitments, giving rise to the so-called 'hump effect' in PESC projections. In each annual survey, the growth rate of government expenditure is typically projected as high for the immediate year ahead, tailing away to much lower rates in the more distant future. But as time rolls on, and the distant future becomes the immediate future, next year tends to become a period of high forecast expenditure—in contradiction of the forecasts made in earlier surveys. This hump effect is shown in the figures of Table III.

Fourth, the PESC system removes control over the *money*

---

[1] Sir Richard Clarke, 'The Long-Term Planning of Taxation', in B. Crick and W. A. Robson (eds.), *Taxation Policy*, Penguin Books, Harmondsworth, Middx., 1973, p. 160.

[2] Foreseen by Enoch Powell, *op. cit.*, and D. N. Chester, 'The Plowden Report: Nature and Significance', *Public Administration*, Spring 1963, p. 15.

[3] D. Galloway, *op. cit.*, pp. 150-52.

TABLE III
THE 'HUMP EFFECT': PESC PROJECTIONS OF THE RATE OF GROWTH OF GOVERNMENT EXPENDITURE,[1] 1970-71 TO 1979-80

Forecast In:	Forecast For: 1970-1	1971-2	1972-3	1973-4	1974-5	1975-6	1976-7	1977-8	1978-9	1979-80	Source
1970-1	2·21	2·16	1·80	2·12	2·30	—	—	—	—	—	*Public Expenditure* 1969-70 to 1974-75, Cmnd.4578, Jan.1971
1971-2	—	2·72	2·87	2·03	1·80	2·28	—	—	—	—	*Public Expenditure* to 1975-76, Cmnd.4829, Nov.1971
1972-3	—	—	6·86	4·65	1·35	1·61	1·28	—	—	—	*Public Expenditure* to 1976-77, Cmnd.5178, Dec.1972
1973-4	—	—	—	7·77	1·41	1·45	1·56	2·74	—	—	*Public Expenditure* to 1977-78, Cmnd.5519, Dec.1973
1974-5	—	—	—	—	9·47	0·99	0·77	1·53	2·44	—	*Public Expenditure* to 1978-79, Cmnd.5879, Jan.1975
1975-6	—	—	—	—	—	2·12	2·49	0·26	0·81	1·38	*Public Expenditure* to 1979-80, Cmnd.6393, Feb.1976

[1] Here calculated as the percentage rate of change from year to year in government spending on a PESC 'cost' basis.

costs of government expenditure because it is planned and committed under this system in *real* terms, irrespective of the money costs that emerge. The PESC projections of government expenditure are all made in the prices ruling at the time of the survey, with an allowance made for a relative price effect resulting from anticipated movements of public compared with private wages and other costs. The unforeseen, although predictable, consequence of this system of planning public expenditure in terms of 'funny money' (as Samuel Brittan has described it) is that government departments have absolutely no incentive to economise on their cash outgoings when it outruns their nominal budget allocation. As they have been given real resource commitments under PESC, irrespective of the money costs, departments 'have been able to bill the Treasury for increases in pay [*etc.*], simply like that'.[1]

Fifth, the five-year horizon of the PESC system of 'controlling' government expenditure creates the possibility that difficult decisions on government expenditure reductions (due, say, to a crisis of overseas confidence) will be deferred to the distant future. Faced with a call for 'cuts', Ministers and administrators in the spending departments are prepared to trade with the Treasury for the maintenance of their current/immediate future expenditure while conceding large cuts on their planned programmes in more distant years. The assumption—evidenced in the 'hump effect'—is that they can later be re-negotiated *via* the application of pressure in Cabinet. 'Slashing' cuts in government expenditure are then announced by the Chancellor to impress overseas opinion. In reality, this represents a *postponement* of expenditure cuts to the distant future. Moreover, they are likely to be reversed as that future draws nearer: cuts are always *manana*. The cuts of £1,100 million for 1976-77 (at 1975 Survey Prices) announced in the Budget of April 1975 were, for instance, more than reversed in the March 1976 PESC White Paper.

Sixth, and finally, the PESC measures rest implicitly on the basic assumption that all government expenditure is on public goods, which must necessarily be financed by government, and which are, therefore, appropriately controlled and controllable by government machinery. An examination of British government expenditure quickly reveals, however, that the bulk of it

---

[1] W. Godley, 'The Measurement and Control of Public Expenditure', *Economic Policy Review*, No. 2, March 1976.

comprises spending on *private* goods in an economic sense, where the more appropriate method of control is the machinery of the market—pricing.[1] The PESC attempt at controlling the bias towards increasing government spending failed for these various reasons, and indeed contributed to that bias in Britain's Keynesian fiscal constitution. In the 1970s, the out-turn of government expenditure has persistently exceeded the intended total. One inquiry revealed a discrepancy of £5.8 billion between the out-turn for 1974-75 and that forecast in 1971.[2] The Select Committee on Expenditure found that 70 per cent of this discrepancy, equal to some 5 per cent of gross domestic product, could not be accounted for by announced policy changes!

The crisis measures of 1976

The Keynesian fiscal constitution reached a critical stage by 1976. Government expenditure had grown by some 20 per cent in real terms over the preceding three years, and had come to account for some 60 per cent of domestic output.[3] The public sector borrowing requirement in 1975 had accounted for some 11½ per cent of total output. The total of new government borrowing since 1971 was now reaching over £31 billion. The PESC system had 'moved into deep crisis',[4] and appeared to be contributing to, rather than checking, a runaway movement in government expenditure and borrowing. All this was set against a background of double-digit inflation, the highest amount of unemployment since before World War II (over 5 per cent of the labour force), stagnant industrial production, and a massive annual deficit of close to £1½ billion on the current account of the balance of payments. Clearly, this situation did not correspond very closely to Keynes's vision of the post-war managed economy as an era of 'joy through statistics'.[5] The Keynesian daydream had turned into a nightmare.

[1] This critique is developed at length in Arthur Seldon, *Charge*, Temple Smith, 1977.

[2] W. Godley, Evidence to the Select Committee on Expenditure, 1st Report, 1975-76: *The Financing of Public Expenditure*, Vol. 2, HC 69-11, pp. 212-3.

[3] On the basis of the 'old' Treasury definition of government expenditure (Table II); the 'new' definition shows a lower figure (below, pp. 68-9).

[4] M. Wright, 'Public Expenditure in Britain: The Crisis of Control', *Public Administration*, Summer 1977, p. 143.

[5] Quoted in D. E. Moggridge, *op. cit.*, p. 127.

Under the pressure of these bleak events, measures were undertaken by the Government to contain the crisis:

(a) Cash Limits on Government Expenditure. In April 1976 a system of cash limits on programme expenditures was grafted on top of the volume limits set by the PESC system.[1] These are administrative limits on the amount of cash that may be spent on specified programmes during the fiscal year. They are determined by converting the PESC constant price programme allocations to money figures, making due allowance for the estimated rate of inflation over the fiscal year. If programme costs rise above the cash limit, volume must be reduced. The Treasury (it is claimed) will no longer meet the bill for the deficiency by presenting a Supplementary Estimate to Parliament. These cash limits now apply to some three-quarters of central government expenditure, and about the same proportion of the current expenditures of the local authorities. They do not apply to those classes of government expenditure where there is a statutory obligation to make stated payments (e.g., state pensions, unemployment and social security payments, debt interest, regional and industrial aid payments).

(b) A Financial Information System. This is an 'early warning system' (first established in September 1975) whereby the Treasury obtains detailed monthly returns on departmental spending within 10 days of the end of each month. For those programmes covered by cash limits the money outgoings are then compared with the planned ones, and any discrepancies have to be accounted for to the Treasury. From April 1977, the monthly comparisons have been complemented with a quinquennial analysis of the volume and money cost changes in the 120-odd major 'blocks' of public expenditure covered by cash limits. Arrangements have also been made to monitor the investment expenditures of state-owned enterprises.

(c) The Redefinition of Government Expenditure. Prompted by critical comparisons between the relative magnitudes of government expenditure in the UK and other Western countries, the Treasury introduced in 1976 a 'presentational change' in the figures. Under this new definition the internally-financed capital expenditures of state-owned enterprises, and those interest payments on government debt which are financed by user charges on government sector outputs, are hencefor-

[1] *Cash Limits on Public Expenditure*, Cmnd. 6440, HMSO, April 1976.

ward excluded from total government expenditure. The consequence is that the ratio of government expenditure to GDP at factor cost emerges as much lower. Under the old definition, for example, the ratio was approximately 60 per cent in 1975; under the new definition the ratio is approximately 52 per cent.

(d) An External Constraint on Domestic Monetary and Fiscal Actions. In 1976 the Government found increasing difficulty in obtaining external loans to cover the deficit on the current account of the balance of payments, and was eventually impelled to apply to the International Monetary Fund (IMF) for a (further) standby of SDR 3,360 million ($3.9 billion). Under the terms of this loan agreement, signed in December 1976, the Government gave commitments to the IMF regarding the maximum size of its borrowing requirement and expenditure, and of the rate of growth in the money supply, for the forthcoming 2-3 years. The PSBR was to be restricted —both in money terms and as a proportion of GDP—to a maximum of £8·7 billion in 1977-78 (amounting to 6 per cent of forecast GDP at market prices), and to £8·6 billion in 1978-79 (5 per cent of forecast GDP). Government expenditure was to be reduced by £1 billion in 1977-78 and £1½ billion in 1978-79 (at 1976 Survey prices) below those planned under the PESC system in 1976. Monetary targets in terms of the maximum permissible amount of domestic credit expansion were laid down for 1977-78 (£7.7 billion) and later years. The IMF constraints on domestic monetary and fiscal actions mean that, in effect, the IMF is acting as an external surrogate for internal constitutional constraints on the government's monetary and fiscal actions.

A conversion of the policy-makers?

The 1976 crisis measures were accompanied by a variety of statements suggesting that there may have been a fundamental shift of opinion in the Treasury and the Government regarding the validity of the Keynesian theory of economic policy. The Chancellor of the Exchequer, Mr Dennis Healey, announced on many occasions his acceptance of the monetarist prescription that the rate of growth of the money supply must be firmly controlled.[1] The Treasury recorded its view that the IMF-required measures would 'on balance improve the

[1] Mr Healey has described himself as 'an unorthodox, neo-Keynesian monetarist'.

prospects for employment'[1]—whereas Keynesian theory would indicate the opposite. And even before 'the (1976) December Measures', the Prime Minister announced his rejection of the Keynesian notion of functional finance to his party supporters in ringing terms:

> 'We used to think that you could spend your way out of a recession, and increase employment by cutting taxes and boosting government spending. I tell you, in all candour, that that option no longer exists, and that, insofar as it ever did exist, it only worked by . . . injecting bigger doses of inflation into the economy, followed by higher levels of unemployment as the next step. . . . That is the history of the past 20 years.'[1]

The outcomes of any set of policies depend, however, not on the professions of politicians or Treasury officials, but on the effects of the measures they adopt. The real question to be asked of the 1976 crisis measures is: *will these measures work* to remedy the basic flaws of Britain's present Keynesian fiscal constitution?

An evaluation of the prospects

First, what of cash limits? This measure does not represent any return to Gladstonian principles of cash control: about 38 per cent of total government expenditure is not subject to cash limits. These uncontrolled elements have been the fastest-growing types of government expenditure over the post-war period. All that cash limits will do is to contain *one* of the glaring defects of PESC—the 'funny money' principle that removed the incentive for departments to seek economies on the nominal magnitude of their costs. The other defects of PESC—the temptation towards 'paper growth', the *manana* effect, and so on—remain firmly embedded in the system of 'controlling' government expenditure.

The efficacy of cash limits in providing incentives to economy in departmental spending will in any event depend on the rigidity with which they are enforced. As matters now stand, a Contingency Reserve has been budgeted for in PESC plans to accommodate proposals not foreseen at the time of the PESC Survey, or which

[1] Information Division of the Treasury, 'The December Measures', *Economic Progress Report*, No. 82, January 1977, p. 1.

[2] The Rt. Hon. James Callaghan, Labour Party Conference Address, 28 September, 1976.

'could not be costed accurately enough at that stage to be included in the expenditure programmes. In addition, Ministers responsible for existing programmes under their control may seek extra provision (from the Contingency Reserve) to meet increases in the estimated costs of their programmes'.[1]

In other words, there are loopholes to cash limits.

More fundamentally, cash limits, like PESC, fail to grapple with the fundamental flaw in the British fiscal constitution—the divorce between government spending and revenue permitted by Keynesian prescriptions and the timing of spending and taxation decisions.[2] Cash limits in no way contain the ensuing political biases.

Second, the Financial Information System is a valuable adjunct to the control system, but, again, it does nothing to check or contain the political biases arising from a Keynesian fiscal constitution. Monitoring public expenditure is not the same thing as controlling it.

Third, the 'presentational' redefinition of government expenditure has removed some of the anomalous features of the old definition, and makes the British figures more easily comparable with those of other Western countries. It may have some internal and international public relations value: British public expenditure now looks much lower to domestic taxpayers and outside observers. And paper cuts in government expenditure are much less painful than real ones, too. But changing definitions does not change real problems.

Fourth, the IMF conditions provide no long-term constraints. As North Sea oil increasingly begins to flow, the current account of the British balance of payments will (ceteris paribus) begin to look healthier. The need for IMF loans will cease—and so will the IMF constraints on domestic monetary and fiscal actions. Britain will then be back to square one—with an unconstrained Keynesian monetary-fiscal constitution. In the absence of constitutional reform, we may predict that the same biases as were witnessed before the IMF loan will re-emerge.

In summary, the crisis measures adopted in 1976 have done nothing to remedy the *basic* defects of Britain's present fiscal constitution. All that they have done, from a long-term point of

[1] Information Division of the Treasury, *Economic Progress Report*, No. 80, November 1976, p. 1.

[2] C. Sandford, 'Wishful Thinking on Public Spending?', *Banker*, May 1977, pp. 47-49.

view, is to paper over the cracks. For evidence to support this conclusion, we need only cite the 'reflationary' mini-Budget of November 1977.

The November 1977 'reflation'

Throughout the Summer of 1977, rumours mounted that the Government was considering 'reflating' the economy, on the 'balloon analogy' of Keynesian thinking (p. 25). These rumours were accompanied by the now time-hallowed tradition of a call by the National Institute of Economic and Social Research (NIESR) for reflationary measures.[1] The Government claimed that the Public Sector Borrowing Requirement (PSBR) for 1977, on the evidence of the first six months, was falling short of the IMF-agreed upper limit by a forecast £2½ billion, and that this gave a 'good deal of headroom' for reflation.[2]

At the September meeting of the IMF, the British Government obtained permission for 'reflation'. Subsequently, in November, a reflationary mini-budget was duly unveiled, with a £1 billion tax cut, and increased social welfare expenditure of £1 billion planned for 1978. This, it was claimed, would boost output and employment. However, as we have recorded, only slightly over one year earlier the Prime Minister had proclaimed that this was not true: that the attempt to 'spend your way out of recession' by tax cuts and extra government spending led only to higher inflation followed by higher unemployment.

How is this apparent inconsistency between the proclaimed beliefs and the subsequent behaviour of the Government to be explained?

A problem of explanation arises only if the presuppositions of Harvey Road are adopted as a basis for the prediction of political behaviour. If we adopt the alternative hypothesis here presented, of democratic politicians as vote-buying agents who seek to manipulate the economy for purposes of political profit,

---

[1] NIESR *Review*, August 1977. A critique of the NIESR's record of forecasting and policy advice, which is of interest regarding Keynes's presupposition (3) (above, p. 49) is in R. Pringle, *The Growth Merchants: Economic Consequences of Wishful Thinking*, Centre for Policy Studies, London, 1976; also J. C. K. Ash and D. J. Smyth, *Forecasting the UK Economy*, Saxon House, Farnborough, Hants., 1974, and G. Polanyi, *Short-Term Forecasting: A Case-Study*, IEA, 1973.

[2] Rt. Hon. Dennis Healey, 'Statement to the National Economic Development Council', 10 October, 1977.

there is no 'problem' of explanation. Our hypothesis allows us to predict that:[1]

(i) the closer an election, the higher the political discount rate on the long-run outcomes of current policy actions, and the greater the likelihood of 'reflationary' measures;

(ii) as tax cuts and transfer expenditures raise real disposable incomes with a shorter lag than increases in government expenditure on goods and services (especially capital goods), the pre-election 'reflationary' increase in the budget deficit/reduction in the budget surplus is more likely to take the form of tax cuts and provision of benefits rather than extra government expenditure on goods and services.[2]

Given that the incumbent British government will go to the country in 1978 (the most widely-touted date being Autumn 1978), our analysis is fully consistent with the apparent clash between governmental belief and action which is permitted by Britain's Keynesian fiscal constitution.

It should not be necessary to emphasise that we do not seek to make a one-sided attack on a Labour Government. Many similar episodes have transpired under previous Conservative governments. The problem here is not that of the particular party in power; the problem is that of Britain's present fiscal *constitution*.

G. Conclusion: 'Folly in a Great Kingdom'

Britain's fiscal constitution is the product of a long process of historical evolution over several centuries. Central to it are certain rules designed to check the manipulations of those in power. Rules have been embedded in the Constitution to constrain the tax-rapacity of a revenue-hungry Crown; others have been evolved to constrain or prevent the misuse or abuse of public funds by corrupt MPs and spendthrift civil servants. These rules have evolved in response to the problems of earlier centuries.

[1] A. Lindbeck, 'Stabilisation Policy in Open Economies with Endogenous Politicians', *American Economic Review*, Papers and Proceedings, May 1976, discusses these points.

[2] This has been confirmed in a study of pre-election manipulation in 26 democracies: E. R. Tufte, 'The Political Manipulation of the Economy: Influence of the Electoral Cycle on Macroeconomic Performance and Policy', Department of Politics, Princeton University, Princeton, September 1974 (mimeo).

But the British fiscal constitution contains a potentially fatal deficiency once the balanced-budget rule is usurped and replaced by the Keynesian legitimation of deficit finance. It retains no rule to prevent vote-buying manipulations of government expenditure and finance by an Executive that has, through the party system, a (working) majority of votes in the House of Commons, despite the experience that the absence of this rule has created grave political and economic consequences. This problem existed in the 18th- and 19th-century Parliaments. It was eventually checked in the 19th century by the constitutional convention of a balanced budget. But, over the last three decades, that vital check has been kicked away by the Keynesian revolution. Yet the danger of governmental manipulation is far stronger now than it was in the 19th century. In 1871, the party divisions in the Commons, where 90 per cent or more of MPs voted in their own party lobbies, accounted for 35 per cent of all divisions. By 1894, this percentage had risen to 76. In the 20th century it has become virtually 100.[1] The possibilities of *economic manipulation for political profit* have become almost complete certainties.

Attempts to contain this bias of the contemporary British fiscal constitution have succeeded only in exacerbating the problem, or in papering over the cracks—of affording a temporary retrenchment. The inherent and fundamental biases and consequences of a system of competitive party politics under a Keynesian fiscal constitution remain. Despite the crisis measures of 1976, these biases will eventually reassert themselves: as they now are.

Sooner or later, and the sooner the better, British democracy must come to a hard reckoning of the political and economic consequences of one of its most illustrious sons, John Maynard Keynes. If it does not, the predictable consequences, analysed in this *Paper*, will continue. There will be a persistent tendency to the growth of state expenditure, and, despite the tax revenues of North Sea oil, the same régime of recurrent budget deficits, and an unremitting and probably volatile inflation that is now, and will continue, to destroy the working of such market processes as remain. How long British democracy and the Mother of Parliaments will survive under the corruption of Keynesianism is an open question. Without constitutional reform their ultimate crumbling can hardly be in doubt.

[1] Lord Campion, 'Parliament', *Encyclopaedia Britannica*, London, 1963 Edn.

In the long run—when, *pace* Mr Keynes, we are not all dead —the British constitution must evolve to deal with the political biases and economic consequences of Keynesian presuppositions about political and bureaucratic behaviour. Either that, or constitutional democracy in Britain will disappear under the strain imposed upon it.

The problem is not one of an 'insufficiency of cleverness', as Keynes so often thought political problems were in essence.[1] 'Cleverness' that avoids *realistic assumptions about political behaviour* is folly. The basic problem to be faced is the structure of *incentives* facing political decision-makers under a fiscal constitution of Keynes's own making.

---

[1] Letter from Keynes to the poet T. S. Eliot, 5 April, 1945, quoted in D. E. Moggridge, 'Economic Policy in the Second World War', *op. cit.*, p. 190.

PART III

Constitutional Options for Fiscal Control

.

J. M. BUCHANAN, J. BURTON and R. E. WAGNER

A. Fatalism versus Reform

This *Paper* has sought to explain why the acceptance of Keynesian economics in a democratic society leads to an inflationary bias, and why the destructive economic consequences that spring from it can make the erroneous Keynesian analysis of our economic order take on the appearance of a self-fulfilling prophecy. We should not be surprised at the contemporary fiscal and economic record. Once the last vestiges of the Classical norm of the balanced budget were removed, nothing was left to constrain the spending proclivities of politicians, and, indirectly, those of voters themselves.

Two means of improvement might suggest themselves. We might acknowledge that policies derived from Keynesian economics cannot be applied within representative democracy. Some might go on to suggest that basic choices on macro-economic policy should be taken away from the decision-making power of ordinary politicians and entrusted to a small group of 'experts', 'economic technocrats', 'planners', who would, it is assumed, be able to 'fine tune' the national economy in accordance with the true 'public interest' and wholly free of political interference. This naïve approach begs all questions concerning effective incentives for the 'experts', and ignores the demonstrated informational difficulties in forecasting and controlling. Various arguments for incomes policies and national economic planning, which now seem to be re-emerging, represent in reality an effort to replace our democratic political institutions with non-democratic institutions more consonant with the Keynesian presuppositions.

From a democratic point of view, there are strong objections to any such removal of decision-making power from our elected representatives. Recognition of the political biases we have described, along with a commitment to the basic values of representative democracy, leads necessarily to a consideration of the fiscal constitution, which defines the set of constraints within which elected political representatives operate. In this perspective, the acceptance of the Keynesian paradigm, misplaced in its analytical foundations, has led to the destruction of one important element of this constitution that has not been replaced. The spending and inflating proclivities that have been unleashed are capable of making the economy appear to conform to the Keynesian view of the world.

[79]

Politicians will be politicians, one might say. And bureaucrats will be bureaucrats, one might add. Together, in the absence of constitutional constraints, they possess enormous potential for economic destruction. Much of the vote-buying activities of politicians have been passed off as necessary to promote a more effectively working economy. And who would want to promote a *less* effectively working economy? But such unrestrained political actions lead to economic instability, which is then used to justify further political efforts to 'stabilise' the economy. So sails the ship of state. To call for further helmsmanship from the pilots who have exacerbated our troubles in the first place would be logical only for those who enjoy being seasick or like long-distance swimming, but it is not a 'remedy' that many of us would anticipate with much enthusiasm. A combination of a rule for fixed monetary growth and a rule for a balanced government budget would go far in checking governmentally-induced sources of instability. Must we continue to trust short-run steering of an otherwise stable ship to an inherently biased helmsman, and then to blame the subsequent instability upon the ship itself?

Force the helmsman to stop fiddling with the tiller?

The prospects for fiscal reform may not seem bright; that should not make us fatalists or determinists. As with the vision of Charles Dickens's Spirit of Christmas Yet-to-Come, prospects look bleak only if existing bad habits—modes of fiscal conduct— are continued. It is precisely because we see not one inevitable projection of history but rather alternative histories that might unfold, and which will unfold as a result of choice and the exercise of intelligence, that we see hope. That hope is that through the explanation of the harmful consequences of present harmful policies we shall adopt courses of action that allow us to escape from them.[1] As people come to understand more accurately the source of the curse that plagues them, fiscal conduct will change. We are engaged in a process in which the explanation of social phenomena alters our understanding of our self-interest, thereby modifying human conduct and social phenomena. We therefore believe that the recent signs of

[1] This theme is stated in Frank H. Knight, *Intelligence and Democratic Action*, Harvard University Press, Cambridge, Mass., 1960, and G. Warren Nutter, *Where Are We Headed?*, Reprint No. 34, American Enterprise Institute, Washington DC, 1975, originally published in the *Wall Street Journal*, 10 January, 1975.

concern about the conduct of budgetary policy under our constitutional framework, of which this *Paper* is one expression and *Democracy in Deficit* is another, will contribute to this needed shift in understanding and, as a result, in budgetary policy.

B. CONCRETE PROPOSALS FOR THE REFORM OF THE BRITISH FISCAL-MONETARY CONSTITUTION

The historic role of the House of Commons was that of opposing a revenue-hungry Crown under the banner of 'no taxation without representation'. It now faces a new challenge, from a new sovereign, and it needs another banner: 'No economic manipulation for political profit'.

What concrete proposals can be offered for the reform of Britain's monetary-fiscal constitution?

1. *A combined budget statement.* Britain is one of the few Western countries in which government spending proposals are considered separately from its revenue proposals.[1] This practice has arisen as the unintended consequence of parliamentary rules of procedure adopted in the 19th century. A change in these procedures is necessary. The two sides of the fiscal situation should be considered jointly, to emphasise the essential link between them.

But this measure would not in itself eradicate the flaws of the present fiscal constitution. It would simply remove a procedural anachronism.

2. *Re- adopt the balanced-budget principle* (preferably in writing). The central problem must be faced squarely. The present British fiscal constitution contains a bias towards persistent budgetary deficits, and permits the manipulation of the economy for short-term political profit. The economic consequences are unremitting and volatile inflation, unending growth of government expenditure, and a continuous erosion of the effective functioning of the price system. If these conditions persist, the ultimate survival of British democracy itself will be at stake.

If Britain is to avoid this grim folly, government must be subjected to a constitutional rule that eradicates its

---

[1] J. Enoch Powell, 'Plan to Spend First; Find the Money Later', *Lloyds Bank Review*, April 1959.

ability to manipulate the fiscal system and the economy for political profit. The rule should also be simple, clear, workable, and comprehensible to the general public. No public purpose is served in beating about the bush on this issue. *The only constitutional rule that fulfils these criteria is the principle of the balanced budget.*

But a return to the previously-unwritten constitutional convention of the balanced budget may not now be sufficient. Mere conventions, once broken, are too easily broken again. A written constitutional rule, rather than a convention, is therefore now called for. The House of Commons must adopt a new Standing Order:

> 'This House requires that total government expenditure does not exceed total government revenue from taxation and charges'.

3. *Automatic adjustment towards budget balance.* Even though required by the House of Commons to adopt a balanced budget, government could present in its Budget Statement only a *projected* equality of its revenues and expenditures over the forthcoming fiscal year. Given the inherent difficulties of forecasting these magnitudes accurately, discrepancies would be bound to emerge over the fiscal year. How then is budget balance to be maintained?

A constitutionally-defined *adjustment rule* is necessary to specify what should happen. If a budget deficit occurs, either expenditure must be reversed downwards to match revenue, or revenue must be increased to match outlay. Furthermore, the adjustment rule must be triggered automatically, by the emergence of a differential between outlay and revenue over and beyond some given threshold. The acceptance of a clear, automatic and obligatory adjustment rule is more important than the specific character of the rule adopted. Our specific proposal is that, if budget projections prove to be in error, and a budget deficit larger than a specified (small) limit emerges, government expenditure must be adjusted downward to restore projected balance within a period of three months. If a budget surplus emerges, the excess funds must be used to retire (i.e. reduce) the National Debt.

The adopted adjustment rule would also need to be codified as a House of Commons Order.

[82]

4. *Orderly transition to full implementation.* To eradicate the budget deficits of recent British vintage within one fiscal year would result in economic upheaval. To minimise these adjustment problems (they cannot be eradicated entirely), the goal of budget balance should be approached in stages over a number of years. Our specific suggestion is that orderly transition requires that annual budget deficits be reduced by not less than 20 per cent in each of the five years subsequent to the adoption of the balanced-budget constitutional rule. Departure from this transition programme would be treated in the same manner as departure from budget balance upon full implementation: the automatic adjustment rule would be triggered. *

5. *Waiver in national emergency.* A waiver clause in the House of Commons Order on budget balance is necessary to deal with national emergencies, such as wars or financial crises. The purpose of a balanced-budget rule is to extirpate the biases and consequences of the present fiscal constitution that exist even in conditions of economic normalcy. It should not prevent recourse to government borrowing under the abnormal conditions of a genuine national emergency. Our specific proposal is that if the majority party (or coalition) holds less than two-thirds of all seats in the House of Commons, the rule of budget balance may be waived if two-thirds of all MPs so vote. This waiver clause would be sufficient to deal with the typical post-war situation, in which no governing party has commanded more than two-thirds of the seats in the House. If it ever did, the waiver clause would have to be strengthened, to restrain the potential manipulation of the economy by the Executive for political profit. Our specific proposal is that, if the governing party or coalition holds more than two-thirds of parliamentary seats, the balanced-budget rule may be waived only if a third or more of the remaining, non-governing-party MPs so vote with government-party MPs.

6. *Conditions for monetary stability.* This *Paper* has concentrated on the fiscal side of the fiscal-monetary constitution. But monetary and fiscal actions are in practice closely intertwined. We have argued for *fiscal* stability; we do not deny that a similar importance attaches to the maintenance of *monetary* stability.

[83]

The Bank of England has apparently moved, over recent years, towards acceptance of the monetarist view that the rate of increase of the money supply should be low and regular. But this change of attitude is not in itself a sufficient guarantee of monetary stability. The Bank has no statutory objectives, and final authority over monetary policy is retained by government, which also appoints the Governor of the Bank. It is these conditions that must be changed if there is to be a credible guarantee of monetary stability. First, the Bank of England must be made statutorily independent of the government, as advocated by the Editor of *The Times*, Mr William Rees-Mogg.[1] Second, the Bank must be required by statute to adopt a fixed and specific rule for the rate of growth of the money supply. As with the fiscal adjustment rule, the precise nature of this rule is less important than the basic principle that a fixed and clear rule is adopted. Our specific proposal is that the rate of growth of the monetary base—the key quantity which determines the rate of growth of the total money supply—should be maintained at a constant rate, equal to the average rate of growth of real gross domestic product over (say) the last three decades.[2]

The House of Commons would also have the right to waive this rule, in times of national emergency, under the same conditions as (5) above.

The difficulty that Parliament faces in seeking to impose these new constitutional rules should not be minimised. For the People's House to battle against an external, privileged minority, such as the Crown or the Lords, is one thing. It must now seek to check a new sovereign that sits in its midst, and which controls it. It is to be hoped that this *Paper* will contribute to that difficult task.

c. UNFOUNDED FEARS

The main worry that some might voice about our proposals is that 'Life without Keynes' would mean a return to the inter-war slump. This fear is completely without foundation.

[1] *Democracy and the Value of Money: The Theory of Money from Locke to Keynes*, Occasional Paper 53, IEA, 1977.

[2] A specific proposal along these lines is discussed by N. W. Duck and D. K. Sheppard, 'A Proposal for the Control of the UK Money Supply', *Economic Journal*, March 1978, pp. 1-17.

First, there is simply no evidence to suggest that market economies are inherently unstable. Econometric research has shown that market economies are dynamically stable.[1] The business cycle does not arise because of any inherent instability on the part of the economy, but apparently is caused by exogenous 'shocks' that disturb its workings.

Second, the evidence indicates that the most serious 'shocks' that destabilise the economy are ill-considered and erratic policy actions *by government*. The tragedy of the inter-war slump illustrates this fundamental truth. Winston Churchill's decision in 1925 to return to the gold standard at the pre-World War I parity has been correctly described as 'the most important single act of economic policy in the decade of the 'twenties'.[2] The massive shock it administered severely destabilised the British economy. This decision was bitterly attacked by Keynes in a pamphlet entitled *The Economic Consequences of Mr Churchill*; to his credit, Churchill himself later came to view his decision as the most serious mistake of his life.[3] The Great Contraction of the 'thirties in the USA likewise owed its origins to inept decisions, in this case by the Federal Reserve Board (the US monetary authority). The historical research of Professors Milton Friedman and Anna J. Schwartz have revealed that from 1929 to 1932 the US money supply (defined here to include time deposits) fell by 35.2 per cent.[4] While some part of this catastrophic decline may be partly accounted for by falling economic activity, there can be no doubt that it was primarily caused by the inaction of the Federal Reserve at the beginning of the episode, and its incorrect handling later on. The Federal Reserve, supposedly designed to prevent banking crises, instead caused one.

The general lesson is that slumps are *not* due to the supposedly unstable nature of the market economy. They are the un-

[1] I. and F. L. Adelman, 'The Dynamic Properties of the Klein-Goldberger Model', *Econometrica*, October 1959; A. Goldberger, *Impact Multipliers and Dynamic Properties of the Klein-Goldberger Model*, North Holland, 1959; B. G. Hickman (ed.), *Econometric Models of Cyclical Behaviour*, National Bureau of Economic Research, 1971.

[2] D. Williams, 'Montague Norman and Banking Policy in the Nineteen Twenties', *Yorkshire Bulletin of Economic and Social Research*, July 1959, p. 46.

[3] D. Winch, *Economics and Policy: A Historical Study*, Hodder and Stoughton, 1969, p. 75.

[4] *A Monetary History of the United States, 1867-1960*, National Bureau of Economic Research, 1963, Ch. 7; this chapter has also been published separately as *The Great Contraction*, Princeton University Press, Princeton, N.J., 1965.

fortunate consequence of external 'shocks' impinging on the economic system: primarily ill-considered acts of government policy.

A régime of fiscal and monetary stability, as here advocated, would not, therefore, restore economic instability. On the contrary: by removing the governmental sources of fiscal and monetary volatility that set off economic contractions, it would reduce the external shocks to which the economy is subject. A balanced-budget policy, combined with a rule for monetary stability, would result in more, not less, stability of the economy.

QUESTIONS FOR DISCUSSION

1. Compare and contrast the Classical and Keynesian visions of the economic order.

2. 'It may be that the presuppositions of Harvey Road were so much of a second nature to Keynes that he did not give the dilemma (between optimal policy choices and the dictates of political survival) the full consideration that it deserves' (R. F. Harrod). Discuss.

3. Analyse the differences and similarities of political competition and market competition.

4. 'Budget deficits are more likely to result than budget surpluses from a democratic choice process that is unconstrained by a balanced-budget rule'. Explain and evaluate this proposition.

5. In what ways may inflation have a disrupting effect on the economy by destroying the co-ordination of prices?

6. Examine the role of the balanced-budget convention in the workings of the 19th century British fiscal constitution.

7. 'The effect of the Keynesian revolution was to remove the linchpin of the British fiscal constitution'. Discuss.

8. Contrast the workings in practice of the Keynesian fiscal constitution in Britain since the end of the war with its supposed workings in Keynesian theory.

9. Describe and evaluate the efficacy of the attempts made to reform the workings of the fiscal system in post-war Britain.

10. 'Sober assessment suggests that Keynesianism represents a substantial disease that over the long run may prove fatal to the survival of democracy'. Examine and critically evaluate the economic foundation of this judgement.

FURTHER READING

Introductions to the developing theory of 'public choice'—the economics of politics—are:

Wagner, R. E., *The Public Economy*, Chicago: Markham, 1973.

Bartlett, R., *Economic Foundations of Political Power*, New York: The Free Press, 1973.

Tullock, G., *The Vote Motive*, London: IEA, Hobart Paperback 9, 1976.

A more mathematically-advanced treatment is in:

Riker, W. H., and Ordeshook, P. C., *An Introduction to Positive Political Theory*, Englewood Cliffs, N. J.: Prentice-Hall, 1973.

Of direct, specific relevance to the topic of this *Paper* there are:

Buchanan, J. M., and Wagner, R. E., *Democracy in Deficit: The Political Legacy of Lord Keynes*, New York: Academic Press, 1977.

Buchanan, J. M., *Public Finance in Democratic Process*, Chapel Hill: University of North Carolina Press, 1967.

Buchanan, J. M., *Public Principles of Public Debt*, Homewood, Ill: Richard D. Irwin, 1958.

Buchanan, J. M., and Wagner, R. E., *Public Debt in Democratic Society*, Washington DC: American Enterprise Institute, 1967.

Wagner, R. E., 'Economic Manipulation for Political Profit: Macroeconomic Consequences and Constitutional Implications', *Kyklos*, Vol. 30, No. 3, 1977.

The Keynesian revolution is treated in:

Stein, H., *The Fiscal Revolution in America*, Chicago: University of Chicago Press, 1969.

The best short, simple guide to Keynes is:

Moggridge, D. E., *Keynes*, London: Fontana/Collins, 1976.

Some IEA Papers on
Aspects of the New Economics of Politics

Occasional Paper 51

Inflation and Unemployment: The New Dimension of Politics

MILTON FRIEDMAN

1977   2nd Impression 1978   £1·00

'I have to warn you that there is neither shock nor horror nor sensation in his lecture, only close reasoning, and a sense of scholarly inquiry . . . I urge readers to buy and read [it].'

Patrick Hutber, *Sunday Telegraph*

Hobart Paperback 10

Not from benevolence . . .
Twenty years of economic dissent

RALPH HARRIS and ARTHUR SELDON

1977   2nd Impression 1977   £2·00

'If one is to hazard a guess about which organisation has had the greatest influence on public economic understanding, it would not be any of the large forecasting organisations with computer models of the economy, but the Institute of Economic Affairs . . .'   Samuel Brittan, *Financial Times*

Hobart Paperback 9

The Vote Motive
GORDON TULLOCK
with a Commentary by Morris Perlman

1976   £1·50

'Professor Tullock's tract deserves our attention because it is disturbing, as it is meant to be. It invites us to consider further what we should be constantly considering—those comfortable assumptions about our institutions that prompt us to shy away from changes that might be beneficial. There is more in common between the public and private sectors than most of us are willing to allow.'   *Municipal Journal*

Hobart Paperback 5
Bureaucracy: Servant or Master?
WILLIAM A. NISKANEN
with Commentaries by
Douglas Houghton, Maurice Kogan,
Nicholas Ridley and Ian Senior
1973 £1·00
'Niskanen argues, with some cogency, that every kind of pressure on a bureau head leads him to maximise his budget.'
Peter Wilsher, *Sunday Times*

Hobart Paperback 1
Politically Impossible . . .?
W. H. HUTT
1971 75p
'The analysis that Hutt offers is a refreshing and succinct attempt to identify the economic consequences of present trends in welfare expenditure, and the political temptations and attractions he thinks are offered by the alternative policies available. He lives up to the strict standards he suggests for his fellow economists in the earlier section of the book.'
John Biffen, *Spectator*

Occasional Paper 10
Markets and the Franchise
T. W. HUTCHISON
1966 25p
'Professor Hutchison follows the course of electoral reform and its effect on economic ideas. He argues that we need to know a lot more about how people's ideas and wants are translated (or not) into political action, and that in any case we need better mechanisms for collective choice.' *Investors Chronicle*

Readings 11
E. G. WEST
'"Pure" versus "Operational" Economics in Regional Policy'
in **Regional Policy For Ever?**
Graham Hallett, Peter Randall, E. G. West
1973 £1·80
'. . . to be welcomed for its appraisal of some of the misconceptions that have grown up around the subject.' *Estates Gazette*

Five Outstanding IEA Books

The Theory of Collective Bargaining 1930-1975
W. H. HUTT

with Commentaries by
Lord Feather and **Sir Leonard Neal**

1975   2nd Impression 1977   Hobart Paperback No. 8   £2·00

'This is a closely argued theoretical book but it makes some powerful and controversial points. Far from agreeing with the conventional view that collective bargaining has improved the lot of the average worker, Professor Hutt maintains that [it] has made the general level of real wage-rates lower than they otherwise would have been, made incomes more unequal, created avoidable poverty and unemployment and encouraged governments to reflate.'

Sunday Telegraph (LEITH MCGRANDLE)

'The workers themselves—or rather, those whose job it is to organise concerted withdrawals of labour—will not take kindly to the Professor . . . his basic case is a sensible one . . . but there can be no simple solution.'

Guardian

'. . . a powerfully-argued economic case . . .'

Liverpool Daily Post (DERRICK HILL)

'. . . Its main theme seems so extravagantly biased against modern trade unionism that it is doubtful whether it will be given the objective examination which it ought to have. And that's a pity.'

LORD FEATHER

'The world of politics and economics . . . needs someone like W. H. Hutt who cares to think about the unthinkable . . . he has pointed our attention not merely to the consequences of collective bargaining . . . but to the fallacies in the basic premise on which the system rests. And he has exposed the sophistries of the premise with irresistible logic and merciless clarity.'

SIR LEONARD NEAL

Selected Economic Essays and Addresses
SIR ARNOLD PLANT

1974   Routledge & Kegan Paul for the IEA £5·25

'. . . at last, a representative . . . collection with valuable autobiographical comments. A great debt of gratitude is due to the Institute of Economic Affairs for having fostered this enterprise. . . . the common characteristics of the whole collection [are] a broad perspective underlying principle, a scrupulous handling of significant detail, and a strong sense of history . . . for the public at large and students in particular . . . a demonstration of how interesting applied economics can be when it is combined with true erudition and practical experience.'

Financial Times (LORD ROBBINS)

'. . . Sir Arnold has [the] Marshallian sweep of theory allied to observation . . . he writes, as he always taught, with a directness that can be pungent. though always laced with good humour . . . his eminent qualities of theoretical analysis and factual description . . . this scholar and pragmatist, whose influence has been out of all proportion to his published work. The Institute of Economic Affairs has done well to assemble this selection of his best thought.'

Economist

'These are all essays of a kind that are sadly rare items in the anthologies of professional economists; for they are deliberately designed to be not merely comprehensible to, but enjoyable for, non-professional readers.'

Economic Journal (PHYLLIS DEANE)

'These essays . . . succeed in interesting today's readers—no small achievement for studies in applied economics written over an extended range of years . . . [they] touch on . . . topics that have recently become intellectually prominent . . . [some] anticipate a good deal of more recent research . . . [others will give] today's reader a few unexpected pleasures . . .'

The Times Literary Supplement (RICHARD CAVES)

The Long Debate on Poverty
R. M. HARTWELL, G. E. MINGAY, RHODES BOYSON, NORMAN McCORD, C. G. HANSON, A. W. COATS, W. H. CHALONER and W. O. HENDERSON, MICHAEL JEFFERSON

Second Edition with an Essay on 'The State of the Debate' by
NORMAN GASH

1974   IEA Readings No. 9   £2·50

'The essayists do not simply rake the embers: they dive into the great crucible of early industrialisation.'

Financial Times (PROFESSOR ASA BRIGGS)

'. . . an excellent contribution to popular education . . . with an important message for those who learnt economic history a generation ago and have learnt nothing and forgotten nothing ever since . . .'

The Times Literary Supplement

'The authors are all serious and reputable scholars and their reports are solidly research-based.'

Economic Journal (PHYLLIS DEANE)

'. . . a valuable corrective to one of the most deeply-rooted historical myths —that industrialisation in England brought general exploitation, working-class immiseration and poverty . . . The authors . . . have provided abundant evidence . . . putting the modern debate on poverty into proper historical perspective.'

The Manchester School (PROFESSOR A. E. MUSSON)

The Economics of Charity
A. A. ALCHIAN and W. R. ALLEN, MICHAEL H. COOPER,
ANTHONY J. CULYER, MARILYN J. IRELAND, THOMAS R.
IRELAND, DAVID B. JOHNSON, JAMES KOCH, A. J. SALSBURY,
GORDON TULLOCK

1974 IEA Readings No. 12 £2·00

'. . . a whole new package of provocative thinking for all of us puzzled
would-be-goods to worry over. . . . Titmuss . . . argued . . . that blood
was not an economic good . . . [and that] the commercialisation of
blood and donorship relations represses the expression of altruism . . .

'. . . now the doubters return to the attack, at a variety of levels. . . . A
lot of the material, particularly the first, more general, section discussing
what people are really doing when they advocate, or rely on, charity . . .
is very sensible and clear-headed. . . .'

Sunday Times (PETER WILSHER)

'The first paper is concerned with the utility derived from charitable
activities; the second with the politics of the redistribution of benefits in
society; the third, fourth and fifth with the anthropology, ethics, and
welfare economics, respectively, of "giving". . . . The second part deals
with the application of such a framework to blood transfusion. The best
paper in the whole selection is by Culyer and Cooper on the economics of
giving and selling blood: an attempt to refute Titmuss's arguments.'

Economic Journal (D. JACKSON)

'. . . a most valuable contribution to the debate.'

Social & Economic Administration (A. J. B. ROWE)

Regional Policy For Ever?
GRAHAM HALLETT, PETER RANDALL, E. G. WEST

1973 IEA Readings No. 11 £1·80

'Hallett opens the batting with a general review of "the political economy
of regional policy" and is followed by a historical review by Randall . . .
[which] is particularly useful and well-presented, and much of both essays
is uncontroversial. Hallett then reviews regional policies in the EEC, and
follows with his third essay on "British regional problems and policies".
. . . Finally, West advocates the blessings of "pure" economics, as distinct
from the more usual "operational" economics, coupled with the "economics
of politics" divided into the "economics of democracy" and the "economics
of bureaucracy".'

Environment and Planning

'Regional policies have for so long been regarded as politically and
economically essential that the need to question the assumptions on which
they are based is often overlooked. Accordingly, the Institute of Economic
Affairs' recent publication . . . is to be welcomed for its appraisal of some
of the misconceptions that have grown up around the subject.'

Estates Gazette

HOBART PAPERS in print

All Capitalists Now GRAHAM HUTTON. 1960 (10p)
15. *TV: From Monopoly to Competition—and Back?* WILFRED ALTMAN, DENIS THOMAS and DAVID SAWERS. 1962 (second edition, 1962, 40p)
16. *Ordinary Shares for Ordinary Savers* RICHARD KELLETT. 1962 (20p)
21. *Freedom for Fuel* GEORG TUGENDHAT. 1963 (40p)
22. *Farming for Consumers* GRAHAM HALLETT and GWYN JAMES. 1963 (30p)
23. *Transport for Passengers* JOHN HIBBS. 1963 (second edition, 1971, 50p)
25. *Education for Democrats* ALAN T. PEACOCK and JACK WISEMAN. 1964 (second impression, 1970, 40p)
26. *Taxmanship* COLIN CLARK. 1964 (second edition, 1970, 40p)
28. *Vacant Possession* JOHN CARMICHAEL. 1964 (30p)
32. *Taxing Inheritance & Capital Gains* C. T. SANDFORD.1965 (2nd ed. 1967, 40p)
35. *Growth through Competition* 'SPARTACUS'. 1966 (second edition, 1969, 40p)
37. *The Company, the Shareholder and Growth* F. R. JERVIS. 1966 (40p)
41. *The Price of Blood: An economic study of the charitable and commercial principle* M. H. COOPER and A. J. CULYER. 1968 (30p)
42. *Economics, Education & the Politician* E.G.WEST. 1968 (2nd imp.1976, £1·00)
43. *Paying for TV?* SIR SYDNEY CAINE. 1968 (with supplement, 40p)
44. *Money in Boom and Slump.* A. A. WALTERS. 1969 (third edition, 1971, 60p)
45. *Gold and International Equity Investment* S. HERBERT FRANKEL. 1969 (40p)
47. *Rise and Fall of Incomes Policy* F. W. PAISH. 1969 (second edition, 1971, 60p)
50. *Industrial Merger and Public Policy* BRIAN HINDLEY. 1970 (40p)
    Hobart 'Special': *Half a Century of Hobarts* T. W. HUTCHISON. 1970 (40p)
52. *Housing and the Whitehall Bulldozer* ROBERT MCKIE. 1971 (50p)
54. *Rates or Prices?* A. K. MAYNARD and D. N. KING. 1972 (50p)
55. *Macromancy: The ideology of 'development economics'* DOUGLAS RIMMER. 1973 (50p)
56. *Macro-economic Thinking and the Market Economy* L. M. LACHMANN. 1973 (second impression 1975, 50p)
57. *A Market for Aircraft* KEITH HARTLEY. 1974 (60p)
58. *The Price of Prosperity: Lessons from Japan* CHIAKI NISHIYAMA, G. C. ALLEN. 1974 (60p)
59. *The Energy 'Crisis' and British Coal* COLIN ROBINSON. 1974 (75p)
60. *Theft in the Market* R. L. CARTER. 1974 (£1·00)
61. *Government and Enterprise* IVY PAPPS. 1975 (75p)
63. *Taming the Tiger* RICHARD JACKMAN and KURT KLAPPHOLZ. 1975 (£1·00)
64. *Experiment with Choice in Education* ALAN MAYNARD. 1975 (£1·00)
65. *How Little Unemployment?* JOHN B. WOOD. 1975 (£1·00)
66. *Pricing for Pollution* WILFRED BECKERMAN. 1975 (£1·00)
68. *Too Much Money . . .?* GORDON T. PEPPER and GEOFFREY E. WOOD. 1976 (£1.00)
69. *Gold or Paper?* E. VICTOR MORGAN and ANN D. MORGAN. 1976 (£1·00)
70. *Denationalisation of Money—The Argument Refined* F. A. HAYEK. 1976 (2nd edition, 1978, £2·00)
71. *Pricing or Taxing?* RALPH HARRIS and ARTHUR SELDON. 1976 (£1·50)
72. *Over-Taxation by Inflation* DAVID R. MORGAN. 1977 (Post-Budget Edition, £1·80)
73. *Poverty before Politics* COLIN CLARK. 1977 (£1·50)
74. *Economic Forecasting—Models or Markets?* JAMES B. RAMSEY. 1977 (£2·00)
75. *Paying by Degrees* MICHAEL A. CREW and ALISTAIR YOUNG. 1977 (75p)
76. *Delusions of Dominance* JOHN JEWKES. 1977 (£1·00)
77. *Can Workers Manage?* BRIAN CHIPLIN & JOHN COYNE; LJUBO SIRC. 1977 (£1·50)
78. *The Consequences of Mr Keynes* JAMES M. BUCHANAN, JOHN BURTON, RICHARD E. WAGNER. 1978 (£1·50)